Immortal Musings

Edited by Liz Thornbury

Poetry by the People
for the People

anchorbooks

First published in Great Britain in 2005 by:
Anchor Books
Remus House
Coltsfoot Drive
Peterborough
PE2 9JX
Telephone: 01733 898102
Website: www.forwardpress.co.uk

SB ISBN 1 84418 415 3

Foreword

Anchor Books is a small press, established in 1992, with the aim of promoting readable poetry to as wide an audience as possible.

We hope to establish an outlet for writers of poetry who may have struggled to see their work in print.

The poems presented here have been selected from many entries, and as always editing proved to be a difficult task.

I trust this selection will delight and please the authors and all those who enjoy reading poetry.

Liz Thornbury

Editor

Contents

The Poems

I Worry

As children grow and do not know
What's in store for them
Who'll explain that after rain and floods?
You must sink or swim

This dog eat dog world we live in
Can be pretty tough
So hard and unforgiving
Where too much is not enough

I worry for the young ones
Who make out, they're clued up
Teenage fathers and the young mums
Whose lives have got screwed up

These troubled times we live in
With anger all around
Where souls who are forgiving
Are so thin on the ground

Why is it so?
I just don't know
Why things are as they are
It seemed when we had nothing
We were better off by far?

Kevin Raymond

Fashion

Fashion decrees that I must buy
A man's shirt with a collar and tie
A minuscule skirt with pleats
Fishnet tights and pinchy shoes for my feet
I know you are thinking, *Don't go there*
But I must and I don't care
For I really must follow this dictum
Because I am a fashion victim

Marion Kelly

The Comings And Goings
Of An Indifferent Mind

If the world were to plunge into nothingness,
Creating chaos, disorder and mess.
There would be only one saviour for my kind
And that's hidden in the deep, dark pits of my mind.

If there was nothing left in the entire planet,
I knew I would be able to forget,
The sinister adaptations of my surroundings,
And retreat inside to create my own ending.

The world that lives inside my head,
Is my haven, while the real world has bled,
Its last drop of blood, but I am blind,
For I am lost for evermore in my mind.

Left to my own concoction,
Reality has been swallowed up and is now gone,
My world is beauty personified,
For once you are able to see my passionate side.

Kimberly Harries

Fallen Fuchsia

Heart-shaped dome above her head,
This crumbling crown of leaves.
They're passing through the colonnade
Now tunnelling a breeze.

Powdered stamens brush her cheek,
These swimming seeds of Eire.
They're floating down the Irish aisle
On autumn's scented air.

Fallen fuchsia at her feet,
These petals strewn to mud
They're buried in the bygone pall
Blood blossoms crushed to blood.

Pamela Preston

Rose

I smelled a rose at Hampton Court
And Heaven knows a dream was caught
In early summer's smiling light
A pleasant scented paradise

As stunning presence halts thy walk
And exclamation fills my talk
I'm rendered helpless for this hour
By Rose's practised flower power

She knew that we could not ignore her
That when she bloomed we would adore her
As her flaunted fragrance works again
She expects no less from us mere men

Dressed in pink and gently swaying
You let us watch as you're displaying
But over fawn or bother you
Your thorns draw blood so think anew

You prove that nature's never blind
But beauty is beauty for every kind
In awe before your sumptuous store
You're remembered now Rose and for evermore.

Raymond Barber

Grief

Grief is an all consuming ache
That tears at the heart,
When from a loved one we have to part,
As time goes on the sad heart mends,
The season of grieving then ends.
The sun shines once more we open the door,
To new loves new friendships,
We never forget the loved one that has gone,
We just move on.

Eileen Patricia Dunn

Holiday In The Lakes

One summer we went to the Lakes,
It really has got what it takes,
To make your holiday dream come true,
With the hills and the vales,
Such a wonderful view.

We walked right up to the top of a hill,
Looked down on the water, so calm and so still,
On Windermere lake, the boats sailed on,
They gently passed by, and then they were gone.

We went on a bus trip, right up the west coast,
Overlooking the sea, and the cliffs it did boast,
At Ravenglass, the road led to the sea,
This was the place, with so much to see.

The little Bridge House built over a stream,
Near Ambleside, the village of dreams,
The waterfalls trickling down through the trees,
The sights of nature, what's better than these!

So put all together the sights we have seen,
The wonderful places where we could have been,
Those beautiful sights, of mounts and lakes,
A holiday dream it most certainly makes.

Iris Covell

In Sickness And In Wealth

Calling all the people, will you ever learn
to place value on importance and not me?
Just how long will you continue to yearn
for my presence in multiple to be
all yours? I cannot guarantee you glee.
Invest me wisely or spend me at your leisure
your quality of life is all mine to measure.

I can help you to realise your dreams, yet to some
I am the dream - a lifetime of total greed
and a belief that with me happiness will come.
No point in continuing to work if no need
just indulge in yourself and increase the feed.
But beware of your friends and their apparent loyal hugs
I'm representing your life through the drink and the drugs.

Priority has no meaning in the world of money
Dying children, atomic bombs, I simply do not care.
I am the medicine in your cupboard, your toast and honey
the clothes on your back and your flesh so bare.
I am not your friend so to ask do not dare.
Just view me with caution and stay on my good side
for I have two faces, one Jekyll, one Hyde.

Susan Macdougal

A Tribute To William Blake

How grand, dear Blake, how vast your sight,
Your scope so universal,
In distant darkness shone your light
So mystical, inspirational!

Your verses touched a young lad's soul
Whose hair is now much whitened,
Your dancing truth helped make me whole
The 'fruit' has mellowed, ripened.

You held the world in a grain of sand
And made the moment holy,
Your spirit roamed in Spirit Land
And grasped the truth more wholly

One question though, unanswered yet,
Churns in my mind most keenly,
It makes me wonder, seek and fret
And begs an answer queenly.

Did He make both the snake and lamb,
Such contrasts most amazing,
Heaven to bless and Hell to damn,
Crucifixion and soul-raising?

If you were here for such discourse,
What insights we could gather!
But you, sweet spirit, plough your course,
And leave us perplexed rather!

Emmanuel Petrakis

Phillipa's Birthday

It was Phillipa's twenty-third birthday
And this chap took her out for some nosh.
Not burgers, or pizza or curry,
But somewhere decidedly posh.

He said that he knew this French bistro
Where the menu's in French - bloody hell.
But just underneath for the thickos
They had it in English as well.

Her date's sense of humour was brilliant,
Joke after joke without break.
When the waiter said, 'Yes,' he had frogs' legs
He said, 'Hop and get me a steak.'

Well, Phillipa laughed and she giggled
Then started to make croaking sounds,
The waiter just grinned as he served them
And topped up their bill by ten pounds.

That bill when it came was a whopper
With extras for this and for that.
And don't forget they were still charging
Her boyfriend for acting the prat.

A birthday event to be savoured,
But one thing does strike her as odd,
He's not took her out ever since then
So why did she marry the sod?

Chris Smith

A Place Of Tranquillity

(The Jephson Gardens, Leamington Spa)

A haven of tranquillity
A solace and a balm
A feeling almost magical
Of restfulness and calm

A place to sit and meditate
And gaze upon the scene
Bright beds a blaze of cheerfulness
With grass a luscious green

A fountain glistens daintily
While overhead the trees
Send down their image dreamily
With gracefulness and ease

No traffic, bustle, noise or fuss
No rushing up and down
How strange to think this world is in
The centre of the town!

Helen M Clarke

Thoughts Of A Pink Geranium

I have a pink geranium,
Who doesn't do a lot,
She leans against the terrace wall
And doesn't give a jot.
'I'll recline here in a semi somnolent manner,
And when the sun rises
I'll just give a stammer of life given by the sun
And then I'll do the honey run!
Aghast and run, all pink and bright,
And give them all a little fright!'

Robert Walker

Happiness?

Happiness is a state of mind
To live life to the full,
But what most people will tell you
Is their life is really dull!

They mope about and grump and groan
And complain, complain, complain!
For them the truth is simple
Life really is mundane!

If only they would listen
And look around as well,
They will find their life
Really isn't a living hell.

That place is where children suffer
Who have no clothes or food,
Thin little mites with nowt on their feet
And you think your life's crude!

Disease and pestilence is rather rife
Their life is not much fun,
Go away and have your moan
If you think your life's done!

They don't have any water
They don't have any love,
But you just stop and think awhile
Cos you have all the above.

Now go away and think again
Of your life that is so dull,
Your present life is not so bad
Happiness is a life that's full!

Belinda Jane James

Live Today

Cannon ball, earthquake, famine and flood
Disease, poverty, peace and love
Charity, kindness, an easy price to pay
For the living to live life for today

For today blest with breath
Yesterday's ghost cast in death
In times of trouble to give peace a chance
Breeze in the sun where daffodils dance

Growth and freedom, pressure's intense
To believe in nothing, sit on the fence
Targeting morels to dig out the mole
For love, happiness, the greater soul

To cast doubt, the willingness to shout
For the belief of your garden in bloom
To understand growth, flower and wither
The flickers of life, dust, disappear
Peace.

R S Wayne Hughes

Lonely Day

Today I'm alone, today I'm sad and blue,
I feel like I'm the only one who ever needed you.
I thought we'd be together 'til we were old and grey,
But then you went, you left me with another lonely day.

I cried my tears 'til they ran dry, I endured my sleepless nights,
I hurt so much I thought that I would never win the fight.
I'm told I'll find him soon, the one who's right for me,
But I already found him, he's just not here with me.

The dreaming never stops, the heartache never ends,
I wish upon a star that we will meet again,
Until that day arrives, my misery will stay,
Wrapped up in my sadness on another lonely day.

Loraine Tebbett

The People's Earth

This is my Earth
I inherited it upon my birth
So who has the right to place borders
And tell me where I can and can not go

We call them immigrants
Those who come to *'our'* country
But we do not own this land
We don't own the right to direct the flow

This is our Earth
We inherited it upon our birth
When did we surrender our freedom
Why don't we ask those questions we all harbour

Like sheep we graze in our master's paddock
Am I the only one who can see the cause
Borders and governments bring about the wars we fight
We are a kept population who silently suffer

This is the people's Earth
We inherited it upon our birth
The lands should be ours to roam
Now we are just nationalities on a divided Earth

We cling to our possessions and money
This Earth though is our greatest possession
How little we care or think of it
Like so many things we just take it for granted

This is our Earth
We inherited it upon our birth
So let's take back control
And learn to act out of love and not fear

Mark A Games

Kindred Spirits

Of lollipop stick longboats
And rollings in grass
Of hunting down conkers
And first day in class
Of pictures in condensate
Captured on glass
And, of wiping the sand from my bum

Reminders of yesteryear
Decades ago
Brought back to my thoughts
By a place I still go
My infantile playground
Where time seems to slow
And such chapters of childhood so come

My firstling adventures, within you, unfurled
First summers, first winters, first springs
You made me perceive a miraculous world
Full of intimate, infinite things

No longer the dusk bell determines your close
And so hastens my exit's commence
From the heart of your spirit
Where everything grows
Unto absolute, relative sense

Show me of somewhere
So perfectly still
Interacting, with nature's applause
And I'll show you Cwmdonkin
The park on the hill
In exactly, the way, that it was

Mark Anthony Noble

When Hope Dies

There no longer burns a bright flame
Just the remnants of an abolished fire
Extinguished by an ocean of tears
The dream - once bright and awaiting the years
Is now a pit of darkness
A dead desire
If only my faith did not tire
And confronted all awaiting fears
Embracing a mission impossible
Climbing higher and higher
The rope on which the future leers
Yet faith, hopes, desires and dreams
Betray my soul as though I have sinned
Trying to cradle you from all possible harm
As though holding a candle in the wind
Yet when the candle is burnt out
Regardless of the eternal tries
Desperately trying to keep it alight
The hope once alive just laughs and dies

Sabreena Hussain

Ally Pally WW2

During WW2 at Ally Pally
Ed Murrow US came up to our war rally
To tell me they wanted to atom bomb Moscow
When I recovered I contracted War-Psycho
Instead of Moscow Churchill got Nagasaki and Hiroshima

In case you do not believe me
I still have Murrow's letter
Not that it makes it any better
Modern poetry never has to rhyme
So long as the truth is told in time
After ninety-seven years my memory is fine

Paff

Fairy Dance

(For Phillippa)

Fairies dance and prance like clowns
In daisy covered purple grounds
With laughing, giggles that resound
Turning and twirling in pretty silk gowns

Daisy chains and pirouettes
With goblin lifts and shuffle steps
Dancing goes on 'til the dawn
Then fairies go to bed with a yawn

The dreams are of next-a-year
When the call to dance is loud and clear
So if you see some flitting light
It will be the fairy dance night!

Kim Taylor

My Pen

It lies here nicely in my hand … its colour blue, the ink is black,
A present from Dad when I passed my exams, oh! a long way back.
Since then, it has written thousands of words and drawn many a line …
Crossed 't's, dotted 'i's, and composed some long letters so very fine.

My hand never ached, my mind never tired
To transcribe my thoughts so wondrously fired.
I now write a book with pen in my hand
A story to tell you - so very grand.

You must wait if it's published, very soon if I'm to be lucky,
All I need now is a good subject, a strong plot that's not mucky …
A tragedy, some laughter, romance, and an ending so thrilling.
But wait! Where's the black ink pot, my pen needs an urgent refilling!

Margaret Kent

Anchor Books – Immortal Musings

Ace High

Cackling with insanity Lord L turned back to his game.
Resplendent in his aura, God looked on the same.

'Poker is my friend,' said one, 'as sure as Lucifer my name
But these cards are against me, look, I've only ace high again.'

'Be still my son,' said the Lord Almighty, ''tis but a game we play.
You should be used to coming last, it's always been that way.'

'You smug old man, how dare you dare, to patronise me so,
This game of cards I may have lost but there's lots more to this show.

One day I shall rise and never stop and vanquish you and yours,
And then I'll sit in smugness while you cringe on all fours.

The Earth shall feel my Devil's touch and Hellfire be the way,
The human race will suffer much with torture every day.

And you I'll keep in my darkest cell to gloat on once a while,
Because my friend, I'm the Devil you know, and your suffering makes
me smile.'

His speech complete, he cast his cards and basked deep in his glory.
The day would come when history books will sing a different story.

'You silly fool,' God unimpressed, 'do you really rule your land?
Such naive thoughts cannot allow to keep all things in hand.

Did you think, when I made you, I'd let you put me under?
So I'd discard all my work and you could steal my thunder?

And what say you of Hell on Earth and of the human race?
Do well would you to stay in Hell, it's such a nicer place.

You see my Eden is paradise lost, these humans just don't care.
I made utopia from my dreams and now there's acid in the air.

So as I said, be still my son I'm sure you're not all bad.
My other boy gives me no grief, but he's much the quieter lad.

And anyway you never know when you can dance and sing.'
And saying such he showed his cards, the highest was a King.

Matt Money

Visitation

I closed my eyes tight that night,
Then had a dream about you
You were standing next to Mummy!
Because she had died too!
She wore a long black monk gown
Pulled down over her face.
I could not see her lovely eyes
She was in so much pain!
She was trembling all over!
Five words she spoke to me,
'Finish the book, our Evelyn
We will always be with you.'
So Daddy please take care of her!
Give her all my love.
You're always here beside me.
Passing on the 'Spirit of Love'

E Riverside

A Perfect Day

Wobbly jelly served with a smile,
Makes having a birthday so worthwhile!
Ten red candles parading on carefully iced cake,
This probably took Mummy hours to make!
A mountain of pressies and all for me
And guess who's invited to afternoon tea?
A distant cousin from overseas,
Sometimes he could be such a tease.
He'd kick my shins and pull my hair,
And nick my chocolates, that wasn't fair!
But that was then and this is now,
Though I can't imagine he's changed somehow!
There's just one thing that would perfect this day,
And that's if my daddy could possibly stay.

Caroline Dean

The Art Of Pondering

People ask me what I'm doing
When I stare into space.
I tell them that I'm pondering,
And truly, that's the case.

I'm very good at pondering,
I do it every day.
My friends think I'm quite crazy,
But who cares what they say.

You can't be charged with pondering,
It isn't termed a crime.
If they gave awards for pondering,
I'd win one every time.

To ponder is a subtle art,
It should be taught in schools.
There's no tricky calculations,
No written hard set rules.

And when I stop this pondering
I still have time to kill.
So, I'll compose another poem,
And test my writing skill.

Brian M Wood

Sad

while summer brings relief
from thoughts of death and grief
and soon the winter creeps
and brings with it the beast

these days I hate and fear what lies
ahead for me beneath my cries
but no one comes and I am left
back with my thoughts
of harrowing death

Mark Dodd

Fruit

Bananas, oranges, mangoes
Pears and peaches too
Full of lots of vitamins
That are good for me and you

Apples, grapes and apricots
Necessary food
Good when dried, good when fresh
Even good when stewed

Some with skins, some without
To remove or maybe not
Chop them up into chunks
And preserve them in a pot

Gooseberries, raspberries, blackberries
Have them in a tart
No matter how you eat them
They're all good for your heart

Whichever fruit you prefer
Dieticians always say
To live a full and healthy life
Eat five portions a day

Neil Warren

Giselle

He closes the door, she closes her eyes.
His footsteps, absorbed by that world outside.
He has come to accept but not understand
her fear of that space, her need to hide.

She walks from room to perfect room,
a castaway's ritual to start the day.
Safe once more from interaction,
no pretence or judgement to get in the way.

On an empty page she creates her world,
controls who she is and where she goes.
Travels to places she sees in her dreams.
Places, 'til now, that no one else knows.

A publishing house values her words.
Her deadline approaching, there isn't much time.
But the manuscript sits alone in the hall,
his mind on his deadlines he leaves it behind.

She remembers the post box across the street.
Panic takes hold as never before.
It hurts to breathe as she fights her demons.
She opens her eyes and opens the door.

Samantha Philo-Gill

My Ungrateful Parrot

Once, in a fun-loving mood
I ventured forth into the game-teeming jungle
A-hunting for wild food.

I came across a wounded parrot
Abandoned and exposed to men and beasts
I felt for it for what fate had wrought.

I picked it up and nursed it with care
Then took it home and built it a cage
I was now ready to tend and to rear.

I fed it well and raised it in honour
Many came and paid, to see my rare pet
Things were very fine, for me the lucky owner!

Later, after days of friendship and of feasts
It sang of cages, of release, of freedom
And cursed the ugliness of men and beasts.

I couldn't understand this sudden change
In my dear bird which was safe and sound
But the world is a place well known for the strange.

One day, after singing itself fully hoarse
My bird broke its cage and took quick flight
Back into the wild, out of my sight.

Sospeter M Shake

Tribute To Mary

(Written 7th June 2005)

There she sat looking old and frail
Some people were wary.
They were blinded by the lady's cancer
But to me she was just Mary.
Difficult at first to disguise my nervy sadness,
My conversation stuttered
However when Mary laughed at my forced jokes
My humble raw bleeding heart fluttered.

I knew I had a job to do now
I had inwardly made a concrete commitment.
Nothing would stop me trying to enrich Mary's final weeks on Earth,
Least of all my disability restrictment.
At times emotions would drench my fake exterior,
So I would say I needed the loo.
After five minutes recomposing myself,
The visit I would wholeheartedly continue.

I was at the hospice for her
No way chasing gratitude.
I just wanted to remind her how to laugh
I achieved this by being rude.
As time is a runaway train that nobody can halt,
The gut wrenching inevitable thing occurred.
Mary lost her battle for breath
However a place in my heart she has reserved.

Darren Mannix

The Window

I am stood watching life through a window,
never involved, never part of the show -
life's cruel game, until I am dealt death's final blow.
The window is open - I can hear voices and laughter -
all this joy that I am never meant to know.
The rivers of tears that I have cried,
all the pain and hurt I've tried to hide -
yet, here I stand; here on the outside.
My tears washed away - unnoticed down the drain.
What did I do to deserve such pain?
People say that the future's bright, the future is great;
most of them, they can hardly wait.
But all I see is a trap that's luring me with fictional bait!
Promises made and broken,
my heart lays bleeding, torn and broken.
I can see the window open,
hear the voices taunting.
I find all the sounds here inviting, yet haunting.
And so, I stand here watching and waiting,
Life looks so good on the other side.

Andrew Dray Fairchild

The Mudskipper

Along the riverbank the mudskipper did a pout
The mudskipper came to a roundabout
The mudskipper gave in and did a rout
Upon finding a jar of sauerkraut
This little fish had to scout
Feeling down with self-doubt
Had to scream and shout
The mudskipper has to sniff and snout
Feeling rather spaced out
After the whale used his spout.

Catherine Powell

My Mask

I put on my make-up each morning,
My mask to face the day,
With it goes the pretence,
That everything's okay.

I've become an accomplished actress,
I smile, I say I'm fine and tell lies,
But if you look real closely,
My smile doesn't reach my eyes.

Does not anyone out there, realise,
What sadness there lies beneath,
Do I have such a good disguise,
That completely covers my grief.

Over the years I must have perfected my guise,
Because nobody enquires within,
But how much longer before my mask slips,
And I will have to give in.

Susan Jenner

Time

Time can stand still, when stricken with fear,
or hurry on past, faster each year,
no room for the present, already the past,
as we sail to the future, a ship with no mast.

Memories soon haunt us, both the good and the bad,
each of them welcomed, no same two ever had,
for what echoes behind us, long it will last,
its essence is future, the present, and past.

'Time - does it matter?' this word made by man,
a concept of age, we count down - we began,
'Flown quick has this year', we state from below,
why worry for numbers, it's in life we all grow.

Dave Woods

I Am Me

What if I was white the same as you?
What if I spoke your language as well as you?
What if I dressed the same as you?
What if I acted the same as you?

Would you want to be seen with me?
Would you want to sit with me?
Would you want to talk to me?
Would you want to be friends with me?

I would like to be seen with you
I would like to sit with you
I would like to talk to you
I would like to be friends with you.

But I am not white the same as you
I do not speak your language as well as you
I do not dress the same as you
I am me and you are you.

Jane Limani

Renaissance

Thank you for helping me see
The chink through the old oak tree
The light through a dark heavy mist
Illuminates the path to heavenly bliss

Now I can walk through the dark
With my head held high
Unafraid
I can reach for the sky!

At the end of the day
When there's nothing to say
I return to the dark and retire
I wait for the sound of the morning lark
You inspire, you inspire, you inspire

S Friede

The Stone

Perhaps five thousand years had flown
Since someone held this stone
Undiscovered where it laid
Until I touched it with my spade
It wasn't gold, it didn't glint
Just a common piece of flint
Though untrained in archaeology
It was obvious to me
I saw at a glance
It was made, not shaped by chance
How basic must have been the life
Of him who made this flinty knife
What was a work of art to me
Was to him utility
The fascination will always last
To find things from the distant past
Men will turn tons of earth
Finding little that's of worth

Vic Calladine

Bread

'When I was a lad,' the old man said,
'Tuppence would buy a loaf of bread,
Freshly baked in the traditional way
Not wrapped and sliced as it is today,
Its warm scent lingering on the air,
Crustily tempting, wholesome fare
When spread with butter and raspberry jam
Or sandwiches of cheese and ham -
A taste of Heaven, a joy supreme
Sustenance of which you dream.

Robert E Fraser

Jill Halfpenny

From Felling this Newcastle lass,
the Strictly Come Dancing class.
The child sure honest extrovert,
Roxie Chicago lady kudos convert.

Kate Mitchell, manicurist polish well,
with Darren Bennett, steps cast spell!
The bee orchid describes well,
dazzling virtuoso star tell.

On Byker Grove and Coronation Street,
now London Adelphi Theatre so meet.
Great actress be Jill Halfpenny,
Geordie has A's and GCSEs many.

At school was rather shy I guess,
to Roxie in black lace impress.
Like Atlanta waltzing her feet,
blue eyes and sweet smile greet.

On ballroom and Chicago show,
brothers Ant and Dec joy grow.
Likes jeans and jacket tweed,
Chicago musical marvel indeed.

Stunner in red dress jive fashion,
While lady Roxie panache passion.
Londoners will adore winsome Jill,
and certain fella Craig such thrill.

G E Woodford

Wartime In Summer (Scotland) - Ashore

The misty morning sunlight
Slanted over the harbour square
Between all the little houses
Together clustered there.
Suddenly a girl was singing
From a room up a twisty stair,
Her voice came sweetly ringing;
A plaintive Scottish air.
Nought else did break the silence
Save a pair of courting doves,
Dipping their heads in dalliance
Among the red tiled roofs,
And in a cobbled stable yard
An old horse stamped its hooves.
Quite alone stood I, enchanted
By the magic of the scene
Until the spell was broken
By a sea bird's raucous scream,
When more came answering the call,
I turned away and wandered off
To the shore by the old sea wall,
Where land uncovered by the sea's hand
Gave a whiff of salt tanged air
From the tawny ribbed and glittering sand,
And sea wrack lines,
By the tide's end there
On the crunching shingled strand.

John Rowland Parker

Untitled

I bravely walked into the canteen
Nothing like this had I ever seen
Lumpy gravy, dried up veg,
'Is that a beetle?' 'No a potato wedge!'

I hold my plate with nerves of steel
Do I really have to eat this meal?
I grit my teeth and ask for fries
They look quite nice, to my surprise!

Fries on plate, I move along the line
The queue is long so I nibble a chip of mine
'These are stone cold!' 'Hey, watch your lip!'
Red faced I shuffle searching for ketchup dip.

'This isn't McDonald's or KFC'
'That I can, quite clearly see!'
No Big Macs here or chicken fillets
Pudding looks like rice with bubbly bits.

I carry my tray and sit and stare
Is there anything edible under there?
When I left school I was four stone thinner
Why did you make me stay at school for dinner!

Jo Patchett

1955

What happened in 1955?
Nearly everyone came alive!
Most people I know are 50 years old,
half a century and celebrating in gold!

Steve, Gillian, Janette, are just a few . . .
even on TV, they are celebrating too!
Paul O'Grady, European Song Contest and ITV1,
so it looks like, there is gong to be a lot of fun!

Electric railways, suddenly arrive . . .
'The Government unveils plans on 25th Jan, 1955'.
Drivers too, had a new Highway Code,
plus updated signs, just for the road!

California's 'Disneyland', opened its gate . . .
where everyone was 'Mickey Mate'!
'SR Toothpaste', was the first advert on ITV,
Florence Chadwick swims The Channel - with a glee!

Cardiff is made the Capital of Wales,
these are just a few of 1955's details!
Were you also 50 this year?
as for me, (in two years' time), said with a tear!

Barry Ryan

No Friend Of Mine

I thought you were my best friend
Until your jealousy got in the way
You upset me so much with your hurtful words
I can't forgive what you said on that day.

It was meant to be an evening out with friends
Not an evening of criticism and jibes
I feel let down and hurt that you behaved in this way
Now I don't want you in my life.

I don't want to be friends with someone
Who tried finding fault in everything I do
I am very happy with all that I have
It's a shame the same can't be said about you.

We live different lives there is no doubt
But you made judgements all the same
I have decided that our friendship is over
And you only have yourself to blame.

Louise Allen

Dreaming

I dream of the stars, the moon and the sea
And of the impossible
That you are here with me
The trees in woodland, could be years ago
But this is for now
And is only your face I know
It's there when I look at the turbulent sky
When the angry weather sees the clouds rushing by
That is the power of nature up above
But your face is always there
This could only be called love.

Anna Moore

Walking The Dog

Walking the dog, freezing cold,
I don't need this, I am getting too old.
The dog's tail gives a little wag,
I am thinking, *What a drag.*
Now we go round the block again,
It's only started to rain,
This isn't a dog, it's a pampered pet,
My will to live had gone, freezing cold, soaking wet,
My neighbour's cat suddenly appears,
By now I am nearly reduced to tears,
Pampered pet shows the cat her teeth,
Puss slopes off, to my relief,
The cat obviously had a fright,
Pampered pet barks with delight,
Something was actually afraid of her,
So now she thinks she is a real hard cur,
Her tail wags so happily,
So does mine, as I head home for a cup of tea.

Maureen Arnold

Bright Red Briefs

I'm the high-thigh guy in the bright red briefs
and I swing down the lane to the sea.
I'm the high-thigh guy posing on the reefs
and the girls cast their eyes over me.

I leap across the beaches, all day long,
then I dance through the waves in my bright red thong,
I'm the high-thigh guy in the bright red briefs,
and I swing down the lane to the sea.

Richard Langford

Albert

Albert Squirrel is my name
Stealing bird nuts is the game.

I run along the nearest tree
To get the bird nuts that are free.

I shin up poles, I walk the wire
Just to get my heart's desire.

The lady of the house gets mad
Because I am so very bad.

Stealing bird nuts is my aim
So they don't have any. What a shame!

I must admit I think it's fun
Especially when I have to run.

I will continue to steal the nuts
Hopefully avoiding those two mutts.

Ann Elizabeth Bruce

Ignorance Is Blind . . .

I lost you once while you were hidden,
Within the threshold of your mind,
Your ignorance was forbidden,
As our thoughts became intertwined.
I told you all that time ago,
They'll play you for a fool,
But by now I expect you're bound to know,
Since their taunts and blows turned cruel.
Through all this time I've become aware,
Of those places you did hide,
It's over now - send your every care,
Out to sea, on the ebb of the outward tide.

Louise Pamela Webster

Goodbye Nan

It's a sad day today
As my nan has passed away
Her last few years have not been good
She was very much misunderstood
That wasn't my nan doing nothing all day
Very slowly wasting away
That's not how I will remember my nan
I will remember the happy times
I know that I can
Picnics, outings, Boxing Day fun
Families together, my life had just begun
So let's not be sad for my nan today
The gates have opened in a very special way
You see my nan is laughing and smiling today
Because my dear loving grampa
Is calling her all the way

Claire Pattison

Me?

Me my master or me my slave?
Me a coward or me so brave?

Me a man with everything to lose?
Me a boy with a path to choose?

Me a lover or me to be loved?
Me an eagle or me a dove?

Me a concept or me a dream?
Me a cynic or me to believe?

Me together or me apart?
Me so near or me so far?

Me, me, me, is that the question?
Please, please, please make a suggestion.

Darren Simon

Trees

I love to go where trees grow tall,
They seem to laud it over all.
Oak tree, ash tree, mighty pine,
That such a majesty were mine.

Their branches ever thrusting high,
Into never-ending sky.
Through summer long a gown of green
For autumn one of russet is seen
In all save the mighty evergreen
For she enchants the Christmas scene

The sycamore and mighty beech
Their branches ever out of reach
In thee our feathered friends find rest
And in thy branches lodge their nest

True peace they bring to mind
Solace to all mankind,
So may I forever see
The strength and beauty of a tree.

Joyce Brown

Summer! What Summer?

Is this the summer, no one can tell
The calendar says that we are in it now
But look outside, where is the sun?
The clouds are grey we can't have any fun
Rain has now started and hailstones fall
Are we going to get a summer at all?
Come on summer let's see you shine
Take away wet weather replace it with fine
Bring in the heat after all it is June
Let's have some hot sun very soon
We need the rain for our gardens to grow
But not everyday as the grass needs a mow
We want hot sultry evenings to sip our wine
Can't do that unless the weather is fine
So don't bring winter yet, it's summer we need
To enjoy the warmth as we dig and weed
Will summer be late or not come at all?
I hope it comes soon, it's too early for fall
Then we can enjoy again the great outdoors
Instead of staying in and doing the chores

Margaret Ward

Snowdon's Crest

From the Royal Goat Hotel's door
On Beddgelert's green valley floor
Where two white rushing rivers meet
And Prince Llewellyn made his seat
Starts a tough trail to Snowdon's crest
That rhododendrons now infest.

Walkers stroll onwards every day
Following this old worker's way
Past faithful hound Gellert's grave pile
To join fine pines marching in file
That shrink, then die, in barren soil,
Rhododendrons, and mining spoil.

Those hikers made of sterner stuff
Will struggle up, and huff and puff,
Racing the steaming rack rail train
Towards the top, come wind or rain,
To join its long gone King hero
Where rhododendron growth's zero.

There pleads Arthur, Welsh poets tell
His blade held in the lake's deep well,
And where now frozen in grey slate
Much older fossils on him wait;
'Don't let your heritage degrade
Through goodness suckers that invade!'

Ronald Rodger Caseby

To August

Oh August!
When e'er my eyes I close to leap
in solitude, prayer or sleep
your image dances before me.
Where! Oh where can I find thee?

Last London chat with you
left on my heart ulcer new.
Long to know if all is well
to my ear your tale do tell.

Have you reconciled that flowing lava
from your erupted volcano thither?
Who's that ape that sent they heart sword?
Where Cupid's arrow sent thee word.

When I smile, I see you smile
when I weep; your tears drop too.
How can I ever forget awhile
the care you lavishly threw?

When in infancy I wept for home
you gave me love to behold
protected me when the den doth open
gave me grip to stand on glue.
Thou art remembered and fondly too.
Where! Oh where can I find you?

Magdalen Chinyere Ogundu

Hope
(For Max)

My life has been tough
but I've suffered enough.
The days of the past
will come to me last.
I'll live with hope
and be able to cope.
For the rest of my days
I will change my ways.
I'll try to be cheerful
and not quite as tearful.
I will try to smile
if only for a while,
cos happiness grows stronger.
So I'll not be unhappy - not any longer.

Pete Ryan

Mandy

My disillusioned dreams of love
lay buried in my heart and
endless time can't heal the pain
that's torn my world apart
my well worn smile is my
disguise with what I can conceal
but with my smile I cannot
hide the pain my eyes reveal
I sit here now with no regrets
and I'll never be the same
as I loved that girl without a doubt
and Mandy was her name

Robbie

Moonlight

I saw her late
one summer night.
With flaxen hair that glowed
in the pale moonlight.
A beautiful white dress
hugged her every swell.
She motioned me to come
sit by her on the well.
She leaned in to
give me a kiss.
I reacted though
something was amiss.
I closed my eyes for
a kiss that did not appear.
I opened my eyes
only to shed a tear.
I was sitting alone,
on the well in the night.
My beautiful lady had disappeared
in the fading moonlight.

Donnie Gillespie

Cricket

I am really enjoying the cricket
Very interesting watching the way they play
It takes me back to all the wonderful
Enjoyable days
You think of the importance of things
Times change and the game is faster
But to me it is the same wonderful game
Of cricket
Perhaps I should go and buy
The book and read up on it

Phyllis O'Connell (Hampson)

Angels

Do you believe in angels? I do,
I met one in October, this is true,
I fell down, and she appeared, and attended to my needs,
I thought she was a nurse you see, as she worked her kindly deeds.

She took me in the chemist, and made a cup of tea,
She bound up all my wounds, and was so kind to me,
And then she brought me home, and stayed with me a while,
She went and fetched my neighbour and gave a lovely smile.

An hour after she came back, enquiring how I was,
I did not ask her name, for I was still in shock,
The next day then, a box of chocolates I bought,
I wrote a note of thanks, to find her then I sought,

Although I asked at the chemist shop, they did not remember her,
I asked another nurse as well, but they looked just in a blur,
No one seems to remember her, although I've sought in vain,
I just know she was an angel, who helped me in my pain.

So I believe in angels, yes I do, and they are watching over us,
Watching over me and you,
The Lord god sends His angels, to help us in our need,
So praise the Lord for angels, in both word and deed.

Ivy Griffiths

Your Oil Painting Of Life . . .

Can you think of yourself as a painting with the designs so unique?
That brings out the best in all of us with the colours that we seek?
We can easily relate to our own individual strokes,
For life is full of many realms, dimensions and teasing dramatic coats.
You can encompass it with the brushes of the many colours of paint,
But you will find that within these colours they will not seem to be faint.
Think of what textures, boldness and brightness of what we
can achieve,
And ask yourself, *What colours can I read in myself, that would really set
me free and believe?*
As we know there are so many techniques, structures and styles,
That treats us in life along with our own different miles.
One colour to another may not bring out the same,
But isn't that the wonder and the beauty of having the title of it to
your name?
So with these thoughts on your mind in this tapestry of oil,
Can you now see the bigger picture of our hearts' own eternal coil?
There are no guidelines, borders or rules by painting over these lines,
So play with your imagination and treasure it until your life's oil
painting combines.
As in life we can now grow to become what we know is true,
And have the experience to share with the many that we touch in clear
full view.

Lee Mak

No Nonsense

I write without meaning no sense meant to be
my chosen nonsense for all to see
where words forge together and spoke without void
they're mine for the takin' I'm so overjoyed
without limit put into auto my wit's on a mission
not dangerous or illegal no means for suspicion
a surprise in each verse unknowing where you're at
until back to reality in two seconds flat
an explosion of thought a muddled mixed mind
a chance to realise my sanity I need find
this reader's confusion is just an illusion
a pattern of words with no real conclusion
so when read by a stranger someone alien to me
I hope you enjoy for it wasn't easy
and no need to explain useless thoughts in my head
as I think it quite good to look back on what's said
but now comes the time to end what's created
at last now all is done I am so elated

T Pickup

Constant Movement

I've sold my space to you.
He's sold his space to me. I'm moving in -
He's moving on, he wants a patio and a tree.
Always a removal van somewhere in the road
Heaving and lifting for someone's next abode.
I hope you enjoy my old space, it's been fine
For me so far but now you've sold me your
Old space I can dine and dance.
I'm driving off now without a second glance.

J W Whiteacre

I, The Wind

The wind is what I am today
On this chilly hot cloudy day
I brush past my problems without a care in the world
I swing my arms with joy as I swirl
Looking down at my many blessings
As I fly over with a heart that sings
I gently caress people's lives
I hope I do, before I die
Birds I carry with their wings
Success and glory I hope it brings
I hope to die, to die I hope
If it creates a death antidote
Death of soul, death of mind
That death will slaughter mankind
Negative vibes I blow away
Making room for sunlight energy coming this way
Just as the sea is clear blue
I am colourfully see-through!

Janan Robin Zaitoun

Acrostic

Round tendrils like the vine
Enfold the silvery wire
Beneath the rose-red sign
Enchantment, rising higher,
Cool clouds are chased away:
Can Orpheus with his lyre
Admit the stars to stay?

Reflect on light whose spear
Earth-bound yet reaching far
Allows the soul fixed near
Delight in distant star.

Andrew Belsey

John

We thought we had forever
No one has forever
I held you close, praying you'd hear
Me begging you to stay, don't leave me dear
I fought to stave off death's dark vale
Feeling helpless, weak, alone and frail
The end was quick and people say
Quick and painless the desired way
You're saved this numb and endless pain
Life will never be the same again
You're all around me night and day
Pushing my buttons in your special way
I watch the clock at half past four
Listening for your key opening the door
Home again, a weary soul
Beat again by just one bowl
I dream you're back again with me
Knowing that will never be
Sleep well my love, we'll meet again
God will decide where and when
We thought we had forever
No one has forever.

Catherine Hislop

Life . . . A Long, Long Road

Life . . . a long, long road, come let me take you aboard,
A pathway where I strode, made by one and only the Lord.
An infinite journey, as sweet as honey,
For a moment I thus repel, to see what the roads foretell.
Of the time gone by, of the time that has to come,
Of the years gone by, the roads just seem to mum.
I don't know what it means, although to learn I am keen.
Who am I? I just wonder,
In the dark. I sit there and ponder.
Oh! These feelings, all so interrogative,
I think to man, these are very native.
So feeling soporific, there I lay,
Looking high up, skywards for a ray,
With folded hands, my Lord I pray,
Oh! Mighty one, show me the way.
Suddenly I see the clouds at bay, and
He showers His blessings on that day.
I propel ahead, I do not stay, while the sun shines,
I will make that hay.
It's a gift to God I repay, in turn He might grant solace. He just may!

Dhwani Doshi

A Quiet Time

Softly but slowly, the noise dies away
Even though it still be the height of the day
The street's busy traffic creeps silently by
Because, in His presence it's just He and I.

How could I miss? For I started so late
Enjoying a friendship He died to create:
I, with my thinking, and praying and reading,
He with His answering, guiding and leading.

I pray for His presence, and feel within
His power victorious casts out my sin.
He speaks to the heart with the message He gives . . .
'In the heart, *your* heart, that's where my kingdom is.'

Therefore, I rise from my knees at His word
For my praise and my prayer He has heard
And go out rejoicing and praising His name
By my actions in life, as the noise starts again.

Jo Allen

School Mornings

The morning is cold
And my bed is so warm
Some poor child's got up
Another ice cube's been born!
We suffer all for a few books and paper,
To curtsey to Miss Smith when you don't even like her
I rise from my warmth and freeze every morning
Another new era of school day is dawning
We put on the horrible clothes that itch and hurt
With their lime-green ties and cardboard shirts
I really hate school, I wish instead
I could stay in the warmth and covers of bed.

Vicky Jones

Muse O'Mine

Ye dancing' sprite for wicked fun,
My muse, her story's just begun
(Sometimes she leaves my zip undone!)
When she twinkles and chatters daily.

She's a wee pixie, she's an elf;
She should have been left upon a shelf
To laugh, amuse her naughty self!
When she twinkles and chatters gaily.

But how is it then that I could muse?
How would I bend and touch the fuse
To explode my dun poetic views?
Less she twinkles and chats verily.

Oh muse o'mine, I love thee well -
E'en if ye damn well please yersel'
To visit, or sit upon that shelf
Where you twinkle and chat merrily.

Mark Murphy

Happy Times

Every time happiness approaches my heart
I would wonder for how long it's going to last
Because time passes by so fast
Bringing the good and the bad moments one at a time
To change my mood's rhyme
Changing it to an uncertain one
And then I would close the curtains
To my everyday play
Simply because I would lose all that I have to say
Losing some stanzas of rich and joyful moments
But the time has come for me to see
Those happy times are there to keep us company
And help us through what bad is to be

Deema Sbeih

After Midnight

Numb and sleepy
Half past four
Don't want to do this
Any more
Waking at night
From thrashing dreams
Watching myself
Fall apart at the seams
Barely able
To hold my place
In the scheme of things
In the human race.

On the cusp that lies
Between Heaven and Hell
Alive in the land
Where fools dwell
Seeking my fortune
Lying in bed
Watching the weirdies
Dance in my head
Hoping for a better
Tomorrow
One where sunshine
Outlast my
Sorrow.

But
I'm numb and I'm sleepy
It's half past five
Pins and needles
Just barely alive
Catching my breath
Where it digs in my heart
Enthralled by my mind
As it falls apart
Encased in the lies
Of the long ago
As you rip
So shall you sew.

Ethel Kirkpatrick

Wide Blue Yonder

The tempestuous sea
Turbulent and wild.
A raging tide
As the white horses
'Hit the waves'
Like tantrums when we
Are not 'behaved'
Sprays of mist
Like a mermaid's kiss
When calm and still
A peaceful haven
On rippling waves
To daydream
Of distant shores
Magic caves
Jewel'd coves
As waves 'lap' the seashore.

Margaret Parnell

Stormy

The clouds are raging in the sky,
A colourless picture of deep grey,
A rip,
A roar,
Of thunder rumbles,
Followed by,
A strike of lightning,
Now the rain pours heavily down,
Pelting against the windowpane,
The warmth of the fire,
A sheer delight,
As I sit in my armchair,
Reading my book,
My mind elsewhere.

Carole Herron

Kiss Of Beauty

Turn off the lamp and I'll still have the sight.
Beauty is a kiss which gives you light.

It's the discovered and rediscovering work going on.
It lights up an internal sun that has freshness of dawn.

'You are so beautiful I am in love with you.'
'Let's get married and I want to be with you.'

It's not the beauty that cause to entice.
Unawareness of beauty in feeling love causes to despise.

'I am an admirer of beauty so I will spend.'
'Make my world beautiful and attractive, use money to no end.'

It's not beauty which ever wanted to start a trend.
It's beautiful, anything like that has many blend.

So what is beauty if I am not right?
Beauty is a kiss which gives you light.

Beauty awakes the dove, which was sleeping inside.
It is a feeling not an owner's pride.

Beauty is in love, in devotion, in nature.
An artist never creates beauty to get social stature.

Beauty is creation, beauty is emotion, beauty is human.
The feeling of its nearness purifies a worldly demon.

So, beauty is not possession and not attraction.
Beauty is a messenger causing holy interaction.

Beauty is the last clue of the enigma to be found.
It's the venue's wand which completes spiritual bound.

Beauty is a kiss, of spirit and His spirit.
It gives you sight as light has no limit.

It completes the eternal ring and shine so bright.
Beauty is a kiss, which gives you light.

Divyamaan Srivastava

First Day

How will it be? I hope I'll see, the ending of the day.
That my pride and sanity will not be blown away.

I'll watch my step; be sure to avoid, any words spoken out of place.
Or awful comment from the room, thrown like a pie into my face.

I'm sure I've packed all that I need, to enable me to survive the day.
But I know for sure, as a fact of life, I'll have left something astray.

A room so full, without but one, to have the sense of two.
If I need assistance at any stage, I just don't know what at all I'll do.

Perhaps if I just stare out of the window, or upon the floor,
I'll avoid being noticed at all, as though I'd not even entered through
the door.

Questions; questions; questions. What will they ask of me?
I'll try my best to answer them, so long as it ain't for some tea.

I see the gate to my fate, being entered by so many more.
But they've each had some practice at this. In fact many a time before.

Boys will certainly be boys I guess, just as girls will indeed be girls.
Though of them both, I can't imply, whom places my rationality in more
intensive twirls.

The time is soon approaching, when the bell to my fate will toll.
My nerves are inspiring a mundane thought. 'I'd be much safer on
the dole.'

Ding ding; ring ring, are the two tones, which the bell
resoundingly makes.
To end the coherent peacefulness when my consciousness
robustly reawakes.

As the door finally opens, my incoherent perplexity disappears.
For to the following inept silence, my intuition emphatically overwhelms
my explicit fears.

'Take to your seats and open your books, to page nine.' What else
could I say?
As I instruct the class; of five-year-olds. 'Well . . . at least now I've
passed the first day.'

Páraic Folan

Our Moral Duty

Let us salute and love heart's divine mind,
Also let us love each true thee that bind,
But no human love should make thee so blind,
Heart is full of tears when seduces mind.

That wraps delight from thee it is sin,
It destroys a thought and beauty within,
How fantasy comes into heart and mind,
It is destruction which do make one blind.

The heartly mind must find the kind of thoughts,
The rightful mind ought to find thoughts that float,
We look for beauty and simplicity,
God wants us to look for reality.

We must feed our heart with delightfulness,
God will be happy to give us blissfulness,
He will grant us full soul of harmony,
Oh, seek that will award us dignity.

I shall love forever the bright beauty,
That will be a believer's duty,
That will make our life sweet joy that will live,
But be soul thy knowledgeable to give.

Milan Trubarac

Love Never Gives Up

Without your love, I have no reason to live,
If I can't make you happy, I have no future to give.
If whatever I do is to no avail,
If I have no love, all my efforts will fail.

Love is patient, love is kind,
A life of commitment for your heart and mine.
Love swallows pride, it endures all things,
Whatever the pain and the sufferings.

Love rejects all evil, for truth love longs;
Love holds no grudges when suffering wrongs.
Love keeps its temper, love tells no lies,
Love views the world from innocent eyes.

Love cannot be selfish and is never conceited,
Love never attacks and cannot be defeated.
Love's strength overcomes even the fiercest reposte,
Love will give of itself, regardless of cost.

To abandon or despair, love will never accede,
Self-fulfilment is love's only need.
A love can drain even the bitterest cup,
In faith and trust, my love will never give up.

Terry Traynor

Echo In My Heart

I hear echo in my heart
To listen to my heart
The soft breeze upon my face
The sunlight in my hair
Summer in the air
The seasons coming and going
The dream upon my soul
I'm searching, looking where to go
I shall follow my heart with God's grace
Today where I'm going
I will start now
The experience just around the corner
My horizon is out there
To take the first step
And believe and receive is waiting for me
My open door, I can taste and smell and touch
And dream to follow my heart
And know with God's direction and will
I can make it out there

Deirdre Banda

To My Cinderella

How lovely you'd look by the kitchen sink
Dreaming of parties, perfume and mink,
Doing the chores each day the same
With hardly a bean to put to your name
And never a thrill to stir your soul
But buttons on shirts and socks with a hole.
Now how would you like to throw it all in
And climb in my car and come for a spin
And revel in caviar, kisses, champagne,
Dance till you're dead but the joy kills the pain.
Your head is spinning with sheer delight
Your body is held in a hold so tight
You couldn't care how and you couldn't care less
Your lips were stolen, you lost your dress.
Your heart is pounding a reckless pace
And love is alight in your lovely face.
But it won't ever happen because of the bores
Of a sink full of washing and a house full of chores.
But dream as you're washing a dish or a plate
If cleaning is chronic, then loving is great!

Chris Porteous

Homesick

Today I spoke to an English girl,
Her laughter made me smile.
I'd forgotten how it does me good,
To flirt once in a while.
It left me quite nostalgic,
Soon as I'd put down the phone,
And I saw with rose-tint clarity,
A vision of my home.

And I forgot the politics,
The lousy rates of pay,
The weather, and the things I have,
That first lured me away.
A storybook reality,
With everything in place,
A world of ordered sanity,
With smiles on every face.
A land so pure and magical,
I simply felt bereft,
Yet knowing I'd not love it so,
If I had never left.

Alex de Suys

Toy Boys

When I came home
From the shops today
I couldn't get in
There were toys in the way.

I clambered over
The living room floor,
And near broke my neck
On the toys by the door.

Into the kitchen
Exactly the same,
Here, there and everywhere
Toys, books and games.

Although I'm not fussy,
And not one to moan,
I'd really like
An immaculate home.

But although these toys
Just make me scream,
Till my boys are grown up
I'll just have to dream!

H B Jones

An Unfortunate Event

Life offers no time to wait on the mind,
To decide what to do for the best.
We will get things wrong and then take far too long,
To step in and clear up the mess.

Fate intervened and was unwilling to leave,
It made no difference what we did or didn't say.
You were destined to move on, and although that felt wrong,
I was meant to carry on my own way.

So let us agree there is no one to blame,
The fault was neither yours nor mine.
It was merely a hitch, an unavoidable glitch,
We got caught up in the same stitch in time.

I just want you to know, after all the sorrow,
I know better than to think of you in spite.
That was just the way it went,
An unfortunate event,
Was to change our lives forever in one night.

Hannah Kate Willcock

Hands

Are your hands taken for granted because they're always there?
Or do you think how wonderful, there is nothing to compare?
Every day they help you to earn your daily bread,
Whether you enjoy your job, or it worries you instead.
Are they slim or chubby with nails painted red or blue?
It makes no difference to the task whatever you may do.
Some hands work for surgeons, they use them with great skill,
Helping all their patients to recover when they're ill.
Fingers on computers, it is no use to moan,
The buttons that you press have a language of their own.
No more shorthand typists, vanished into the 'blue',
Laptops have taken over, please tell me is this true?
Some hands work for mechanics servicing vehicles of every kind,
Their hands are mostly oily, but they do not seem to mind.
There are pilots flying planes way up in the sky,
Boeing 747s for folks like you or I.
Some hands alter dresses for figures large or small,
To save us buying new ones when going to a Ball.
I could go on forever, so friends please do beware,
And *always* treat your hands with *'tender loving care'*.

Esther Hawkins

Black Widow

Swathed in black she beckons you
wicked widow out to woo
an unsuspecting male or two
ensnared by love are they

Soft she calls thro' still night air
'let me take you to my lair'
others warn them - boy, beware
if hunter turns to prey . . .

Passers by will sympathise
as one more victim drops and dies
cocooned within her web of lies
a crumpled corpse beside her

L'amour is such a cruel game
yet those in love all do the same
and only have themselves to blame
when failing for a spider . . .

Kathryn Atkin

Precious Time

Time so fleeting, earthquakes tumbling
Down whole town communities,
Life so fragile, nations crumbling
Problems and hostilities,
Powerful teachers, earthquakes teaching
Peace in Heaven's sovereignty,
Mankind humble, journeying reaching
Outward to eternity,
Time so precious, blessed and given,
Mercy streams from Heaven above,
Mankind fearless, peaceful, shriven,
Faithful, trusting in God's love.

Lorna Troop

What Is A Mate?

He'll wait for you when you're two hours late.
Pop around on your birthday, with the beer in a crate.
Stand on the terraces, singing those songs of hate.
A boozy weekend without him, hard to contemplate.
Lend him some money, the repayment can wait.
Then, along came Carol, my one and only soulmate.
But, she married my mate, so at the church gate, we all did congregate
And I was left to pass around the plate.
In time, I was called Uncle by his kids, just a surrogate.
Now, I sit alone without a mate.
Staring forlornly, a TV dinner on my plate.
I hear he is now pushing up the divorce rate.
I hate my old mate, but me and Carol's relationship is starting
                                                    to formulate.
So, now it's all over with my old mate
I believe, he's got a fella, all those years and I thought he was straight!

V L Round

Listen . . .

When we turn away from Him to pursue our selfish ways
Seeking only Earthly pleasures, laziness and wasted days
Avert our eyes from those who need us
blind to beggars' outstretched arms
or children, hungry, poor, neglected
trapped by this world's evil charms
Then ignore the people's crying, babies killed for pity's sake . . .

Do you think the Jesus in us would be proud of us today?
You and I we know the answer and the course that He would take
Lord forgive us - we pray

Barbara Harrison

Mr Parsimonious

When there's a collection,
He's got no change,
But anything for free,
And he moves into range.

He'll sign the card,
Vows to pay you later,
About as much chance of that,
As he'll tip the waiter.

When it comes to buying rounds,
He either stands at the back,
Or rushes to the toilet,
With a diarrhoea attack.

Even if he doesn't like it,
If it's going for nowt,
He will ram it, down his throat.

If he goes out for a meal,
He doesn't want to split the bill,
Reckons he's not paying his share,
Because the food has made him ill.

He's very good,
At branding others 'tight',
Deflects the attention
From him being a parasite.

Though eventually
People catch on
And now avoid the 'parsimonious' one.

Keith Large

Thoughts Of You

You were the cushion to soften my fall
You were my light in the dark
You were the air that tasted so sweet
You were the one who stole my heart
You were the sunshine on a foggy day
You were the cool summer breeze
You were the first daffodil in the spring
After the winter's freeze

You were the lush soft green grass
You were the first star at night
You were the gentle autumn fall
You were the hand that held me tight
You were the cool refreshing water
You were the sky so blue
You were the gentle kiss of rain
You were the morning dew
You were the colour in my life
You were the sound of the ocean waves
You were the one who made me feel strong
You were the one who was brave

You are the one I will never forget
You are the one that's in my heart
You will be in my thoughts till the end of time
I wish we never had to part
You are the one who I miss the most
You are the one who made me cry
I will remember you for eternity
We should never have said goodbye.

Naomi Humphries

Roots

In years gone by with grime and soot, my existence would be doubtful.
But now with air that's much more clear, my chance of life is hopeful.
Although my roots have no firm base, I cling to life with verve.
But in this lofty, lonely home, my only friends are birds.

'The wind' that once was my friend, and bore me to this height,
Is now my constant tormentor, and blows and swirls with spite.
My fear is that as I grow, my roots will not support me,
And I shall crash down from this place; will you be there to mourn me?

They say that all of humankind needs oxygen to live,
And all the trees throughout the world; this they gladly give.
The lungs of this planet, or so they say, are forests like the Amazon,
And from where I sit, I do my bit although I'm only one.

I fear my time is getting short, how long can I survive?
Nutrients up here are poor I fear, and for these I constantly strive.
As I look towards the park, a deep longing yearns within me.
If the wind had blown another way, then who knows where I'd be?

Below me stands a place of worth, where students come and go.
Where eager faces frown or grin, each enthusing just to know.
Where knowledge is gained, by young and old, from a
broad curriculum.
In this place of worth, this scholar's home, this athenaeum.

I have watched it grow, from strength to strength, putting down
its roots.
In sold ground but unlike me, who can't support my shoots.
Exams passed, qualifications gained, pride and joy abound.
I have observed it now for a few short years; but how much longer
will I stand?

I need some friends, some kindly souls, people who could assist me,
To take me down from this hard brick mound and hopefully
relocate me.
I don't want much, just a bit of ground, to stretch out root and branch.
So scholars all, rally to my call, and please give me a chance.

John Robathan

Mica And Doogie

This is a story, I hope you will like
It won't give you nightmares, nor give you a fright
It all starts on a planet far, far away
Called *Zeg-a-zee-boo-boo*
That's a hard way to say!

It's not far from Mars
Its neighbour is Venus
And many have said they have popped down to see us
But don't worry if you haven't met
Neither have many others . . . well . . . not yet

Well this particular alien is full of fun
And likes to makes friends with everyone
Her pet is called Doogie, he's covered in hair
Full of fun and always there
Well Mica . . . she's about 4 inches tall
And against the others, the most smallest of all

She has a big round nose, nearly as big as her head
With funny shaped ears and electrodes of red

She'd jump in her spaceship
With Doogie her pet
They'd pack all their goodies and then they'd be set
With a rumble, a shake and a big pow wow
All co-ordinates are ready for they are now off

They arrive at the planet that she knows is Earth
As she has all knowledge from the day of her birth
She'd fly street to street in a hope she might find
Children awake when it's their bedtime

Then there in the distance
They'd see a night light
So they'd slow down their spaceship
So not to give them a fright
Mica's and Doogie's eyes fill with delight
'Do you think they're awake?' Well . . . let's hope that they're right.

Dominica Kelly

A New Day

As I lie here and soak in my hot tub of bubbles,
I close my eyes and float away from all my troubles.
Cacooned in penetrating warmth, relaxed and silent,
Just the music of bursting bubbles, that tickle my skin
and send tingles within.

This must be the nearest to Heaven, like floating in space and time,
A transition of this world to the next,
Nowhere near as complex as people might think.

Relaxed and supported your mind turned within,
Peace and contentment, no goals in life to win.
Yet of course it's my bath and the water goes cool,
The bubbles all burst and I really do have loads of goals.

So out I climb, dry and dress myself,
Look out the window and try to figure out how to achieve
my Earthly wealth,
Never forgetting to say thank you for my health,
It's a new day.

Janey French

Faces

Faces come and faces go,
But the faces that matter
Are the faces you know
Faces may come in January
Disappear by December,
But the faces that stay
Are the ones you remember.
Some faces push, some may shove
But the faces that care
Are the faces you love.

H C Williams

Redundancy, Reluctantly

There's no more work here mate,
They've closed t' factory gate.
Go down t' job centre,
Your details you will enter.

Thanks very much Al,
I thought you were my pal!
I've worked here 30 years,
Didn't know it'd end in tears.

So this is finally it.
On my butt I refuse to sit.
I'll go find work today,
I've got to pay my way.

Have you written a CV?
Have you filled forms X, Y, Zee?
What is all this jargon
Just to drive a ruddy wagon?

I've still got my pride,
And refuse to be taken for a ride.
I'll spend my redundancy,
Founding my own company.

Then again, it's good intention,
But of the sum, there's been no mention.
Life's like a roller coaster,
This job lark, I'll have to master.

I've enjoyed life to the full,
The past has never been dull,
They say life begins at 50,
For now I'll have to be thrifty.

David Goodlad

Goodbye Tears

(For Luke)

I can't believe where time has gone
I hate to say goodbye,
To a man who stole this girl's heart
It almost makes me cry.

Yes, I will see you very soon
But that doesn't stop these aches,
Candy canes and alcohol
Can't and will not take your place.

I'm not looking for a substitute
In any way, shape, form or size,
I only want you in these arms
You make every wrong seem right.

You are the light that guides me
The only truth that I can see,
But most of all I'm thankful
For the love you shine on me.

Baby boy, you're one in a million
Your strength could make me cry,
Yet again I'm missing you
For we just had to say goodbye.

Jennie Hope-Kirk

Thy Beloved Face

I behold Thy face before me, dear Lord
Everywhere that I may look,
In every star that shimmers from afar,
In the pages of my book.
In the flames that flicker upon my hearth,
In the waves pounding the shore
In each summer, winter, autumn and spring,
And all that has gone before.
In the centre of a beautiful rose
Thy beloved face I see.
In each autumn leaf embraced by the breeze,
Forsaking home on the tree.
In the sun whose warmth caresses my face,
In the wind ruffling my hair,
In the sand protecting each step I take
I see Thy face everywhere.
As time is now, and before it began
Thy face was there to behold
Before the Earth was peopled, my Lord,
Before diamonds, before gold.
And I know, my Lord, when my time is come,
And I kneel on bended knee,
As my heart overflows with love, my Lord,
Thy beloved face I will see.

Ellen E Stephenson

Older Star

Sit by the fire and think no more
Of hair now turning grey
Or of the beauty you once had
Time now slowly takes away

Instead just think back to the days
When you were at your best
And how that star that I once knew
Did shine much brighter than the rest

Those eyes so bright yet shadows deep
That held a love so true
Some men would gladly sell their soul
If they could then have you

I've seen the changes slowly come
As we have passed on through the years
Now when I look into your face
I know it holds for me no fears

For every change that time has done
I have kept my own true score
The greying and the lines that come
Just make me love you more

So cuddle closely by the fire
And curse how time flies by
You're still to me a brighter star
Than any in the sky.

P M Stone

A Sailor's Farewell

I had left you at the break of day
that's how it had to be.
To Portsmouth dock to join my ship,
was where I had to be.

That night, I watched the moon's reflection
luminescent, flickering across the sea,
and in the restless waters heard!
La Mer's haunting song, a symphony.

Just like those sailor men of old
I had to sail the briny.
To feel, the sting of salt in the wind
with the bright North Star above me.

A merciless mistress is the sea,
not one that I'd ever sought.
But I couldn't resist when she beckoned me,
for like a fish in a net, I was caught.

Just as the waters ebb and flow,
The seven seas I must roam
but though they take me away from you,
in time they will bring me home.

One day, I shall leave the sea behind
that's how it has to be.
And I'll find you waiting at the dock.
For the sailor, home from the sea.

Jo Mackenzie

Memories

Can you remember days gone by
When schooldays meant a shirt and tie?
And, when the morning bell did ring
Assembly hall, then hymns to sing.
The classroom, with its blackboard
And rows of wooden desks
The inkwells, pen and paper,
Books, jotters and the rest.
The duster for the blackboard
Made out of wood and felt
The teacher's stool and table
But worst of all, the belt.
Times tables we repeated
Spelling and grammar too
Today we're told old-fashioned
Be modern, bright and new
Forget the past and ancient ways
Get children better taught,
We're in the new millennium
Yet here's a sober thought,
If grammar, maths and spelling
Are irrelevant and bad
Could that explain why lots of kids
Can't read and write or add.
The powers that be must realise,
That learning in the past,
Had already stood the test of time
And still today does last.
Perhaps, instead of modern ways
High standards should return
And those who advocate all else
Should from their posts adjourn.

I A Morrison

The Cowboy

He walked into the saloon and looked round,
Men in large hats and boots, a merry sound:
'How do, Pardner,' the usual greeting,
Smoking pipes, drinking and eating.

The music started and a dancing girl,
Swished her can-can skirt as she did a twirl;
The longing started all over again,
The girl had been more than an old flame.

He turned his attention to his old mates,
Put the past behind, forget his mistakes:
'The usual, Harry?' called the landlord,
An expensive drink, he could well afford.

'Don't look so sad,' a wise old Indian,
Advised this tall and handsome young man:
'I shouldn't have come back,' Harry replied,
To the friendly Indian at his side.

'That girl was young and foolish then,
You wanted to see your friends again:
Harry, this town is where you belong.'
His next words were drowned by the lady's song.

'It was no fun being jilted,' said Harry,
'By the girl you love and want to marry.'
'I think you should give her a second chance,'
And Harry sighed, as he watched her dance.

She suddenly stopped, what an occasion,
The crowd waited in anticipation:
She smiled at Harry, looked into his eyes,
What happened then, was a complete surprise.

Diane R Duff

The Challenge

'Move two degrees north,'
Said the Commander of the ship.
'No,' said the recipient
With a merry little quip.
The senior repeated it
But was no farther on
For the answer came, 'No,' again,
The intention was gone.
This time it was an order,
Barked at the young sailor,
Again the challenge was refused
As he went two shades paler.
'I am a battleship
Of tremendous length and girth.'
'I don't care how big you are,'
Said the sailor with mirth.
'I am an Admiral.'
'And I'm an able seaman
But whatever you choose to say
I can act like a demon.'
'Why can't you move?' the Captain asked,
'You're as mobile as me.'
'No I'm not, whate'er you say -
I'm a lighthouse you see!'

Rita Hardiman

Drive To Arrive

Be you one of the fair,
Who use the roads to get there,
And if you drive, do take care,
Of other road users be aware,
Positive action can set the scene,
No need to think of what might have been,
Respect the law, it is for all,
Whether stopping, starting or answering the call;
Traffic lights are for control,
Properly used, no accident toll,
At pedestrian crossings, do give way,
Courtesy to others, for you to display;
The maximum is the speed limit,
If you exceed it, then trim it,
Or an accident you may cause,
Don't rush it, take a pause,
Keep your distance, not tailgate,
Braking time can secure one's fate,
Switch off your phone, it does distract,
Concentration helps you react,
Think before you act,
Or not, make it a fact,
For the safety of all just strive,
And bear in mind,
Drive to *arrive*.

George Beckford

Foxglove

In a forest deep where beasties sleep
Where centipedes and crawly things creep,
In the treetops high,
Halfway to the sky,
Foxglove, the elf, would frolic and leap.

Reaping their harvest in field and dell
The wild bees knew him and knew him well.
They gave him honey,
Golden and runny,
In acorn cups or a walnut shell.

Foxglove's delight on a moonlit night
Was giving the owls and mice a fright,
Riding on a hare,
Its back sleek and bare,
O'er heath and moor like a bird in flight.

His summer home was an old crow's nest
With feathers lined and one of the best,
When winter blew cold,
Or thunderclaps rolled,
A hollow tree gave shelter and rest.

R Smith

Relevant Rhyme

Relevant rhyme is the replication to irrelevant rhyme
Couplets dropping from the inner depths of my mind;
By the day diction and repertoire is steadily growing
While the lyrics, gimmicks and verses keep on flowing.

I don't duplicate, replicate but I initiate and recreate
Originate and create verses sweeter than chocolate.
Irrelevant rhymes grate when I communicate
And don't elevate when I orate and disseminate
Immaculate gems to those who truly appreciate -
As lyrical renegades relegate the irrelevant to waste.

Relevant rhyme is more than the poetic minds' designs
But words of truth and wisdom often have a reason;
Be it love, move, sooth or bode signs of the times
As they transcend trends, continents and seasons.

Keep it compact and write to make an impact
To counteract the abstract art by counteraction,
And see it practised in annihilation not observation.
Writing for form not fun subtracts from what you impart;
Make a resolution to the nation to show your intention.
Get into the act and show fact and tact in this poetic pact.

Joseph T M Nthini

The School Run

It's eight forty-five, the brigade's on its way,
For it's the start of another school day.
Mothers with pushchairs and small children in tow,
Hogging the pavement in an orderly row.
Excited youngsters leave their mother's side and run,
Chasing each other and having such good fun.
Amidst the noise, the bustle and the clatter,
The parents are having their morning natter.

Outside the school, car parking is a chore,
Most want to park outside the school door.
Parking down side streets and on the village green,
Churning up grass, spoiling the picturesque scene.
Cars blocking driveways, house owners in a spin,
Unable to get their cars out, being blocked in.
Contacting the headmaster to make a complaint,
Ringing their employers to explain why they are late.

The playground is full with children running amok,
Five minutes to go before the doors unlock.
Impatient parents who have work on their mind,
Need to be off and leave their *cares* behind.
The teacher's whistle blows and silence ascends,
The children form an orderly line, playtime ends.
Into the place of learning they slowly track,
In the sure knowledge, their parents will be back.

K H Watts

07.07.2005

You shared our shock, you shared our pain
Things will never be quite the same
Terror unfolding on TV
Carnage in London for all to see
Al-Qaeda claiming they had done it
The reason? To disrupt the G8 Summit
Discussions to try and end world poverty
Help poorer countries be debt-free
Gleneagles a meeting for world peace
More talking and talking that fighting must cease
You can understand people saying why get involved
No matter what's decided, nothing ever gets solved
I'll no longer donate money to any charity abroad
Especially to countries that live by the sword
'Charity begins at home,' they say
It certainly will do from today
Another saying also comes to mind
'Don't bite the hand that feeds you'
Don't pretend to be blind
Think of Great Britain, not what's best for Bush
Give it the elbow, give it a push
The G8 concert went down very well
But after what's happened who can tell?
All the good it created now washed away
Remembering what happened on this sad day.

Martha Ann D'Souza

Innocent Grief

I wanted to play
but you'd gone away
Mummy was crying
Grandma was sighing,
'What will you do
now you are two?'
I held Mummy's hand
tried to understand
why she was sad
and where was my dad?
She patted my head
Said, 'Go back to bed,'
Gave me a smile,
'I'll be up in a while.'
I climbed the stairs
Knelt for my prayers,
'Dear God in the sky
Do you know why?
When I wanted to play
You took him away.'

Jan Hedger

Secret Mission

Come in Sam Shaw
You go today
At half past four
Your code is
Are you the Irish joiner's wife?
Your contact will say
Yes my name is Patio doors.
Good luck Sam Shaw
You may have drawn
The short straw
But don't slam the door.

Geoff Carnall

London: 07.07.05

Send me a tragedy
Here is a verse
When you think things are bad
They turn for the worse

Hell on the Underground
Hell on a bus
Why do these idiots
Make such a fuss?

The whizzbangs go off
They crump and they kill
But they won't change a thing
And they never will.

For London still turns
The flowers still grow
The pigeons, the starlings,
The Thames will still flow.

We do things our way
It's our country my friend
We grumble, we argue
But it's ours to the end.

Martin Harris Parry

Caressed

An angel dropped a star from above
To show us we are Heaven blessed.
To put a zeal upon our love
And our souls have been caressed.

M Wayland

Oh Lord

Oh Lord to You we kneel and pray,
Keep us safe by night and day
So we may stay true to You
In everything on Earth we do.

Oh Lord to You we kneel and pray
In our hearts You'll always stay
While we're awake and not asleep,
Help us O' Lord Your commandments keep.

Oh Lord, to You we kneel and pray,
Showing You our love in every way
In You dear Lord we put our trust
That You will forever stay with us.

Oh Lord to You we kneel and pray;
Help us to be good this day,
To love and help one another,
Treat everyone like sister and brother.

Francis Allen

Destiny

From the first frozen moment in time of loss,
To the powerful yearning in time of grief,
I question Fate's own cruel eye,
And Death's swift hand, like a heartless thief.

From a partner's warmth in mutual love,
To the cold indifference of life alone,
I curse the weakness of humankind,
And Fate's decision when the dice is thrown.

From good deeds done and friendships forged,
To a speechless, helpless dying form
How are we chosen when to go?
Perhaps predestined, when we are born?

Ann Pickering

Cathedral

The angels smile their stained glass glow
Upon the priests muttered incantation;
And the crypt is a home of deathly cold
For the ghosts' silent supplication.

Masoned walls suffused with sorrow
For the sorrowful whisper many moans.
The chill air creeps in like a bad omen,
This place of all souls and their lost bones.

The floors hold the tombs of the dead,
The vaults weighed with a thousand confessions.
The alter intones a truth supposed
Priest unholy in his crow back beckons.

So offer up your pleading prayer
To the shadows suffused with menace,
For God to grace your expectant heart,
Faith needs intangible to bed the faithless.

Kay Smith

Husband

Love is powerful. Love is true
This is how I feel about you
You make me good, you make me strong
You make me feel like I belong
You make me smile, you make me laugh
You are my present, future and past.
I love your smile, your mouth, your lips
From your head to your toes, to your fingertips
I love you so much and for evermore
It is you that I adore
I just wanted to say thank you for making me your wife
And for you, husband, I pledge my life.

Angela Oldroyd

Black Eyed Peas!

(Dedicated to my son Aaron Wilson age 10)

A playground trip on the floor!
What next to greet me I was unsure!
A football goal was in mind,
The blow that hit me was unkind,
First the floor, then his knee,
A big, black eye was given to me,
The swelling large, my eye black,
A hospital trip on track.

First the doctor, then the nurse,
A bottle of Calpol will fix this curse!
Blood-red, swollen and black,
The love for football, I'll be back on track.

Gaynor Wilson

It's Nostalgia

Life starts when you're forty,
Well that's what they say,
And fifty's not bad
In a funny old way,
At sixty you feel just a little run down,
So you charge up your batteries
And light up the town,
Three score years and ten
And you just reminisce,
About journeys you've made,
And the signposts you've missed,
Now ten more years on
With such memories to treasure,
May this birthday be one
You'll remember for ever . . .

Joan Hammond

Tears Down A Vase

Do flowers feel pain
When pulled from their roots?
Do they miss air and rain
And the gardener's mud boots?
Do they miss summer days
When the sunshine is out?
Do the leaves lose their glaze
When the blooms aren't about?
Will the blooms miss old Bumble
And the sweet butterfly?
The leaves when they tumble
From the trees that're so high?
So does anyone know then
Do all flowers cry?
When they're cut from their stem
Do they fret, then just die?

Shirley Jones Dywer

Reputation

Beware the adjective 'superb',
keep adverbs consistently on ice.
Avoid metaphors for kin and colleagues;
brief sentences, no clauses, be precise.

No raised eyebrow of the cynic,
be open, no coded secret wink.
Speak only when spoken to,
avoid gossip; take time to think.

When friends insist on sharing troubles.
Listen to their every word, don't prod.
They'll clothe you in a mist of seeming wisdom
and a reputation only given to a God.

G Melia

The Supremos

You won't have the jitters
When these kitchen fitters
Are assessing and checking the scene
They will be on the job fitting units and hob
The best that you've ever seen

So please make some space
For Paul and Jayce
They not only fit but supply
When they are in motion, it's total devotion
They really are ready to fly

Their work is supreme
They are simply the cream
And 'Coppenall Kitchens' the name
They will board it and brick it
Their work rate is wicked
A class act and one awesome team

While others are spouting
They are tiling and grouting
But it really is money well spent
With real satisfaction a fantastic reaction
The customer feels real content

So if you are itchin' to have a new kitchen
I can heartily recommend these
When they're on a winner, they go without dinner
It's the customer first, if you please.

Esmond Simcock

Come Rain Or Come Shine

They all head for Glastonbury
On a hot, sunny day
Hats of blue, pink and yellow, red and grey.

Packs on their backs a heavy load
Trampling along the busy road
All heading same way, Worthy Farm
The sun is shining but for how long?

Up go the tents, wow, what a sight!
Is this living it up for a couple of nights?
Queue for the loo and for a wash,
Nothing up-class and nothing posh.

It's for the music we come, year after year
And also companionship and we shout and cheer.
You may be aware that the skies will shed tears
But we're used to that now, mud up to our ears.

We slip in the mud and laugh and shout
Glasto without mud wouldn't be Glasto, no doubt.
We're here! We're here! For the time of our life.
Sweethearts and partners, husbands and wives,
Swarming like bees around the hives.

So swing it Mr Music Man and we'll clap and cheer
It's just about over for another year
We'll all meet again one day in June
When the sun is high and a bright, bright moon.

So cheerio now, I'm starting to toot
What's that stuck there? Gosh, my wellington boot!

Rachel Mary Mills

Fate

Two men met at night
On a plane mid-flight
As one is prone to do
They talked till the day was new.

Being of a similar mind
There were many things to find
Like work and wives
Travel and lives.

And as they spoke they saw
Their lives were joined by more
A face with dark, doe eyes
That had caused many lies.

Secrets were now shared
Souls were bared
As their pasts dissolved
Their guilt took hold
Of the night.

Karen Disney

Auboud

The smell of your skin,
sunlight warm
upon my cheek:
Am I awake,
or merely asleep?

Keith Alan Deutsch

O Sacrum Convivium

(Dedicated to deceased: Pope John Paul II and my father, Mr Gerry Mooney)

Holy sharing of life, O Sacrum Convivium:
Easter week, on a Maundy Thursday:
O Sacrum Convivium: in Tunisia
At night, the sparrows are asleep among
The palms of Hammamet, North Africa:
O Sacrum Convivium: a gently
Lighted swimming pool is a babbling brook,
In the dark, splendour under the stars,
Of a full moon, a wondrous sight,
O Sacrum Convivium: O Holy Banquet,
Easter week on a Holy Good Friday,
O Sacrum Convivium: Holy sharing of life.

Edmund Mooney

Website

Good morning, garden spider,
my best delight today,
I marvel at the way you work
though never getting pay.
You spin throughout the morning,
and even well past noon,
when I retire to blissful sleep
are you spinning by the moon?
Patience is your virtue,
much wisdom you accrue,
however smart we think we are,
for you there's nothing new.
I salute you, heart-shaped friend,
your cream and coffee hue,
when we are all past self-destruct
you'll spin right at the end.

Malcolm Williams

Me And You And All Humans Too

Their conscience, does not bother them,
Their conscience, rather small,
I'm sure, in fact that they have not,
A conscience at all.

For they never really curse the dark,
And they never praise the light,
And they're always in the thick of things,
And they always stir the s****.

And in their eyes, if you look deep,
Behind the sight, a conscience weak,
As pilot said, as he watched Christ die,
His conscience, blamed the other guy.

Sometimes they're vain, but never deep,
Sometimes by God, they make me weep,
They always fall, between two stools,
But really, they are only fools.

Sometimes they're quick, they're never slow,
Sometimes they're yes, but mostly no,
Sometimes they're blind, but they can see,
They're often you, sometimes they're me.

And in their voice, if they speak deep
Behind the sound, a conscience weak
As pilot said, as he washed his hands
Our conscience must, be built on sands.

A Power

Marriage

Marriage used to be the goal for all
But today its sanctity is in free fall
Our leaders' examples fall short of required
With divorces and living together admired

Many couples shy clear of taking their vows
And asking them why just leads to rows
Quite happy they seem to enjoy married pleasures
Without the commitment to married life's measures

There are many others who did the vows give
To being together as long as they live
Celebrating their wedding as years flow on past
Silver, ruby, diamond - long they may last

No one's pretending married life's always rosy
Nor are they claiming such life is all cosy
But working together to iron problems out
Is a key feature on life's roundabout

To couples who hesitate about marriage vows
Don't be afraid about serious rows
These will occur whether married or not
But belief in the vows should avoid a walkout

The sacred state of husband and wife
Should be the basis of all family life
A protective shield within which you can bear
Your children and keep them protected from fear.

Archie Livingstone

Skipping Rhyme 2005

Clitter, clatter,
Hear the patter
As we go out to play.

Clitter, clatter,
Getting fatter,
'More chips' is what I say.

Clitter, clatter,
Idle chatter,
Mobile phones are quite OK.

Clitter, clatter,
How we flatter,
'Celebs' most every day.

Clitter, clatter,
We all natter,
Keeping thoughts away.

Clitter, clatter,
Now we scatter,
Junk that's here to stay.

Clitter, clatter,
What's the matter?
We've forgotten how to pray.

S J Dodwell

My Head Says . . .

My head says *Get out of bed*
My body is not so keen
The alarm is incessantly ringing
My pillow's a welcoming screen.

My head says *Get up and go*
My body can't seem to move
I knock the clock off the table
I've got to get in the groove.

My head says *Now is the time*
My body has to comply
I've to shower and go to work
Or the day will pass me by.

My head says *Never mind*
My body is coming round
I'll just have to go with the flow.
The radio's a rousing sound.

My head says *That can't be right*
My body shudders in disbelief
It's reporting news at 4.30am
They both say, *What a relief*!

My head says *Do something useful*
My body says *Go back to bed*
With another three hours to snooze in
My body wins over my head!

Mary Wood

Can't Ever Make Me Flawed

I am not a piece of garbage,
nor am I worthless junk,
I'm not a toy for you to play with
or a wreckage long-time sunk.
You don't have the right to hunt me
then to shoot me in the back,
or beat my body black and blue
so I make that mirror crack.
You can't rearrange me, break or change me
or tear my spirit out,
'cause you're the one who cannot love
the one with all the rage and doubt.
You see, I was made a perfect diamond
a priceless jewel to be adored,
and not you or anything you do
can ever make me flawed.

Andrew Hobbs

Sly Fred

When you took ten pounds from me sly Fred
For a clock to wake me up said Ted
I thought it would be
An alarm clock said he
Not a broken clock to beat me over the head!

Joan M Wylde

Piety Versus Terrorism

A distance has formed between us
An invisible barrier impossible to breach.
I've reached an impasse in my emotions
Too afraid to stretch out and reach,
For God with all my unsaid words.
The situation has become absurd.

The breakdown in our communications
Has left me reeling and stressed.
This lack of love that I'm now feeling
Has left me alone and depressed,
My prayers it seems are now not enough,
I feel like I've been nailed to His cross of love.

This is punishment for my self-doubt
For a belief that has gradually subsided.
It now feels like my credo is on trail
And the jury has returned undecided,
Each day my faith gets a little more blown apart.
Each day I fail to see the goodness within man's heart.

Keith Tissington

A Chance

When you know it's over and the time has come to part,
You must be brave and face the truth and say what's in your heart.
The flame of love that once so bright is now a little spark,
A glimmer of its former self just glowing in the dark.
But just hang on it's not to late this marriage we could patch,
The flame of love will burn bright again, has anyone got a match?

Mick Gayfer

How Odd

It's fourteen hundred years or more
   since Saxons heard of Jesus Christ,
Augustine came to win them o'er
   from Woden, Thor and more sufficed.

The pope said, 'Let them keep their ways
   of making merry now and then
but do it all for Jesus Christ -
   His birth till death for fallen men.'

But did he think in all these years
   that weekday names would still so thrive
that Thorsday, Tiwsday, Freyasday
   would still be used and Norse survive!

Who are the Christian heroes great
   to give their names to names of days?
So honour give where honour's due
   and not to pagan gods give praise.

But what of other faiths at home
   would they all wish to tolerate?
T'would lead to bitter rivalries
   and lead to tensions on a date.

But one source lies within our world,
   the sister planets to our Earth
so Venus, Neptune, Saturn days
   would be joined by Pluto's birth.

But, wait a mo, these planets too
   were names of Grecian gods like Styx.
We'll have to call them numbering
   as Threeday, Fourday, Fiveday, Six.

Owen Edwards

Roller Coaster

Let's ride the roller coaster of life
It takes us up and down
We never know what lies ahead
To make us smile or frown

At times you're in a tunnel dark
When nothing will go right
You struggle on until the day
You emerge into the light

Starting out, do you recall
That early snail-like pace
And the feeling of excitement
Of what you were to face

Then suddenly the ride speeds up
And time, it flies so fast
And you wonder where the years have gone
When you look back on the past

Nearly halfway down the track
But no time for feeling blue
Got to think about those things
You still would like to do

But that's much easier said than done
With so many choices to make
And still the ride goes faster
Can no one find the brake?

The reality is therefore
That you can't hold back the tide
So let's not look too far ahead
And just enjoy the ride

Michael Digby

My Mom

Mom, when I see how you are today,
I often weep - occasionally pray,
Remembering our happier times gone by
Give mixed emotions - I smile - I cry;
I question why you suffer so,
Why a mind so alert, is now so slow?
You used to look so lovingly at me,
Now can you remember? Do you even see?
Mom, sometimes I'm selfish,
I don't want you to go,
The pain I feel, I love you so,
Yet I know, all your confusion would cease,
And death would be such a marvellous release . . .
To be able to hold you still, makes my day,
Yet so much pain, when I have to go away,
Everything in God's world happens for a reason,
Like summer and winter,
A happy and sad season,
All will be revealed in the passing of time,
But why? Why? I cry - you committed no crime,
I do remember your smile, your joyous laughter,
I comfort myself, it will be again,
In the hereafter . . .

Chris Perrins

PC Illiterate

I'm the first to admit that I can't work a scanner
My printouts are all of a blur
I can't seem to figure out how to download things
My data will never transfer
My floppy discs mangle when I press to save
My system tools point blank refuse
I can't get my hard drive to even start up
It's not that I try to misuse
I log on correctly; my password's spot on
I sit there and stare at the screen
I click on my mouse when I'm prompted to do so
I try to respect my machine
So why won't it just let me type out a letter?
Or log on to AskJeeves.com
Before it implodes, or explodes, or shuts off
Whilst corrupting my new CD ROM
I see other people just typing away
Without any need for assistance
Yet I can't pass go, cos my hard drive's too slow
It must be the worst in existence
There's no hope for me . . . I'm just not PC
In future I'll write things by hand
Bill Gates is to blame, for this moment of shame
I think the whole thing should be banned.

Bee Gordan

Cradle Song

Lay me in a cradle
from the bough of a mango tree.
May the skies smile away
all my saddened tears from me.
May all the clouds
pillow me on moving hues
warming me.
May the sun drown me in kisses
tiny, tiny flowers blooming.
May the breeze
brush bright blushes,
scented of mangoes,
ripe and red.
May the leaves bustle, rustle,
rocking carrying tales
from scented fields.
And the birds
chirp around guarding
as I sleep on dreaming.

Dr Mary Annie AV (Anna Maria)

Hatred

Two Great Spirits enter our life,
The Great Spirit of Evil, causing disaster and strife,
The Great Spirit of Good, we should all adhere to,
To hate no one at all, may no one hate you.

Hatred is the tool kit of the Great Evil Spirit,
Tools of mischief, damage or sorrow every minute,
The Spirit of Good is not easy to hold,
Those that can are brave, gentle and bold,
The fruits of Good are nice children and love,
Regardless of religion or Heaven above.

Roy Kimpton

Second Eternity

An instant can be an eternity as I watch or gaze,
The child wrapped in his game gets lost in the haze.

The old man sits the same each day
And the dog is sleeping every which way.

We race or we glide, but time stays the same.
A second is between heartbeats, lose or gain.

When I dream, time goes slowly by,
The more we watch the seconds surely fly.

And when I sleep, whole hours go fast
And when I'm awake do those moments last.

Alan Bruce Thompson

Proverbial Errors

He who laughs last may well laugh most long,
Horrid cackles fading into feeble frog like croaks,
Slowest by far in perception of simple jokes.
Could this proverb grammatically be quite wrong?
If many hands make light work, in troth,
How come too many cooks spoil the broth?
Mankind may sup canned soup at little cost,
Unless he who hesitates has, the tin opener lost.
Wisely should not one look before one leaps
Into deep debt which then grows exponentially.
Better by far, neither borrower nor a lender be,
Thereby, both sanity and solvency one may keep.
Truly, if the soul of wit be brevity,
Here I conclude in time for tea.

Anne Omnibus

Sweet Talk

Mary had a mobile phone,
And it was red and green,
The very brightest telephone
That anyone had seen.

She always had it with her,
Talking day and night,
And in the village where she lived,
Was a familiar sight.

But the postman called one morning,
As he sang his little song,
Clutching an 02 bill,
Ninety metres long.

Mum and Dad so furious,
Sent Mary off to bed,
And when they took her phone away,
Many tears where shed.

She's still seen in the village,
Her hand glued to her ear,
Chattering like she did before,
It's sad no one can hear.

Elaine Beresford

Catapult

My mind is like a catapult
If flicks from here to there
Though nobody can see my thoughts
They know they're always there

My head is all frustrated and
Pleasant thoughts get less and less
In fact they turn to nightmares
Something I dread and must address

I feel just like the matador
Who is running from the bull?
I should turn and take them by the horns
And expel them from my skull

I know I should find peace some day
Though what I need I seem to ignore
I do not want to fear this way
Peace have I been searching for?

I have arrived at my conclusion
A happy future isn't slight
I will compress all my ill feeling
And catapult it with my plight.

S C Matthews

A Human Problem

An orphanage - a secret room.
A little girl goes to her doom
Unknown to me, unknown to you.
What can we Western people do?

For little Suzy is Chinese,
And to conform with policies
Parents must have one child, not two.
What can we Western people do?

A 'health food' which comes from Shenzhen
Fills everyone with life again.
It's foetus soup or foetus stew.
What can we Western people do?

They pick up pregnant girls in carts,
Sterilise them and break their hearts.
They give folk forced abortion too.
What can we Western people do?

They fund atrocities like these
Out of our taxes, if you please.
Create a fine old how-d'ye-do,
That's what we Western folk can do!

Jillian Mounter

Take Me, Take Me

Take me, take me
In your arms and hold me
Look into my eyes - what do you see?
Sweep me, sweep me
Off my feet and we'll embrace
For the love so strong in the human race.

I love you, I love you
In many words I can't say
For my love for you in so many ways.
Kiss me, kiss me
And tenderly put me down
For my love for you is a crystal crown.

Look into my heart
Your name is engraved in love
For you my darling are my treasure throve
Hold me, hold me
And kiss me once again
And our love will last forever.

I love you so much, no words can explain
I love you, I love you, again and again
Kiss me, hug me so we will remember
The last dance The Waltz will be forever.

Raymond Duncan

Be Certain

Close your mind and accept the lies,
Never acknowledge your own surprise.
Be ever apathetic and know it's wrong,
And tell yourself it won't be for long
Be inconspicuous and keep up the pace,
Ignore the fact you're just another face.

Make it clear that nothing could hurt you that much,
And flinch at every human touch.
Just forget the image once before your eyes,
And seal up your heart, until it dies
Block out any reason that might come your way,
And make sure you're the one who gets their say.

Be extra careful that once you see sense,
You put on a mask, and keep up the pretence.
Make sure that whatever form you take,
It could never be construed for anything fake,
Make certain you can keep it up forever,
In every situation and whatever the weather.

Lucy Bradford

The Rose

Yesterday evening I came across a small mountain ahead of me,
as I drew near this mountain,
I saw what appeared to be bags upon bags of all sizes;
piled up with various machine parts,
and cardboard rolls, all piled up high,
Right at the top of this mountain of rubbish,
my eyes fixed on what looked like a flower.
I had to take a closer look,
but how could I get close without bringing it down,
and shedding its petals all around!
Then I suddenly remembered that I had my binoculars in the car,
quickly I yanked them out of the car;
took the dust caps off, and holding them up,
I looked straight at the mountain of rubbish in front of me.
I adjusted the lens, and there it was,
'Wow!' Not only was it a flower,
but it was a lovely rose out in full bloom.
Here in the mist of people's rubbish,
was a lovely sweet rose pouring out of its fragrance all around;
Falling like sweet incense to the ground.

T Gibson

The Child

A child must have your love and care
Until it is full grown
And everyday, must have full share
Of happiness alone.

No hurt - no fear must this child know
Each day a pleasant day
And as with love, you watch them grow
You learn then, how to pray.

You pray that life will treat them fair
That they will know true love
For others, they will learn to care
Reach for the stars above.

You do your best to make them whole
To face the future strong
For as you know deep in your soul
You cannot go along.

So just for now it's left to you
To give them happiness
To do the best that you can do
You cannot give them less.

Gordon Andrews

One Morning At Church

I sat in the church the other day,
Hymns were sung and we knelt to pray.
Very clearly was the lesson read,
An announcement was made, for someone to be wed.

The choir seemed to be in excellent voice,
Sang an anthem of the minister's choice.
For the Holy Communion I did not go,
I read some hymns that I used to know.

Those hymns I read, I thought were fine,
Excellent in metre with a beautiful rhyme.
I gazed round the church at the pillars so tall,
And the high vaulted roof that covered us all.

In the congregation I saw many a white head,
I thought, 'What will happen when they're all dead?'
It seemed to me, like a Senior Citizen's Club,
Who'll fill their places when they're in Heaven above?

My life has seen a lot of good things die out,
Streets now seem empty with no one about
I ask. 'Have people just lost their desire to pray?
Will churches in future, slowly pass away?'

Albert E Bird

Gooseberry

I am a gooseberry, sweet and yellow
In the suns' rays I ripen fast
Then I fall to the ground below
Food for insects, I will be at last.

I am a gooseberry, bright and green
Hard and sour, unfit to eat
Any who try, it will soon be seen
Acid in stomach, will then repeat.

I am a gooseberry, just right for picking
Shaking, dissolving, and breaking I am.
Then in a saucepan, with sugar, I am sticking,
Becoming red, pure, beautiful gooseberry jam.

I am a gooseberry packed in a jar
Kept in a fridge for some future ate
Jar opened at some time, on a day now afar
Served then with custard, upon a large plate.

M Hubble

Flynn

Your colour is of pirate's gold
The deepest shade ever told
Your mane and tail for all to see
Matches autumn leaves to me
Eyes as dark as any soul
You must have been a handsome foal
Nature kind no vicious streak
I'd recognise those stocking feet
A heart as big as any tree
You were surely meant for me
As we grow old, this thing I tell
You're one thing I would never sell

Lesley Hartley

Anchor Books – Immortal Musings

A Happy Event

(Biologists estimate that orang-utans will be wiped out in the wild in the next decade. News item, The Times)

To 11-year old orang-utan, Hsaio-Quai,
at Wool, in Dorset, (Monkey World): a child.
Hosannas for the babe's nativity -
caged, safer than he would be in the wild.
When, with our son, we went to Sandakan
and stood beneath the dripping canopy,
we watched a family of orang-utans,
summoned, come down to feed and drink and play
in Eden. Madonna's offspring groomed
as on the trees monsoons fell steadily.
We could not know such innocence was doomed,
nor guess how soon this troop would pass away.
Since man is unregenerate and cruel,
let us proclaim yesterday's birth in Wool.

Norman Bissett

Rainbow Colours

Rainbows to carry in your heart
Their beautiful colours will never part
The magical feeling that fills the air
Giving a sense of not wanting to share

Holding the colours way deep inside
The indigos and violets go passing by
The reds and oranges hold their glow
The yellow shines so bright you know
The green falls down onto nature's Earth
And the blue is from Heaven to light up the Earth.

The wonderful gift that we have been given
We can hold in our hands and keep as a vision

L Wall

The Rock

I am the rock to which they cling,
The one to whom their troubles bring,
But even rocks are known to crack,
And who is there to bring me back?

Advice and love, I give it free,
But who is there to comfort me?
In darkest night and lonely time,
I have no strength a rock to climb.

Voices crowd a mind so full,
A puppet feels the strings that pull,
I often yearn for strings to break,
But there are those I can't forsake.

Their trust I have, I cannot fail
And despite all I will prevail,
A friend I am and so shall stay,
A love, my own, maybe one day.

A rock, my own, to which I'll cling,
And to her my troubles bring,
A love to find that will not crack,
She'll be the one to bring me back.

Sean James Olson

How Went The Day

Tell me something I don't know
A painful heart - and tears flow
How many anniversaries can love give?
Yet sleep the night, please forgive,
Sorrow stands, in motion - day and night
We think of you! Every day till the light
Brings another question and so,
Dad! Why did you have to go?
The pain has gone - within your heart
But our pain is at the start
It starts with tears - ends with a loss
Daily we grieve, what price the cost?
The cost is losing someone we love
Yet I know he's smiling up above
Still I know the hurt and the pain
In our lifetime will forever remain
How went the day? - It was hard
Yet we read each sympathy card
Each line says what people know
That we love you lots but it's time to go
Go where? With your heart on your sleeve
Dad! Forever with us - as we grieve.

Lee Connor

Eric Griffiths

Pre Beatles were The Quarrymen,
Lennon went to Quarry Bank High School,
In 1952 in the same 'house'
As Eric Griffiths and Pete Shotton, cool!
Lonnie Donegan's music inspired them,
To form a Scouser Skiffle Group,
Called themselves The Quarrymen,
They were no Boy Scout Troop!
Rehearsed at Eric's mum's house,
In 1957 at a Wootton church fête,
Paul McCartney met John Lennon . . .
The rest is history, mate!
In 1958 George Harrison
Supplanted Eric on guitar,
In 1959 they disbanded . . .
Eric didn't get 'that' far!
He joined the Merchant Navy
Until 1964.
Next he joined the prison service
For thirty years or more.
In 1997 he was invited
To The Cavern's 40th birthday,
Reunited with Peter Shotton . . .
A Quarryman replay!
Rerecorded 'Come Go With Me'.
That John Lennon sang yesterday
When Sir Paul McCartney met him . . .
What more's there left to stay?
Eric Griffiths died in Edinburgh . . .
Just the other day.

Jësu Ah'So

Once

Once I saw a little fly
Skimming all the trees
Didn't look that big
'Bout the size of two fleas.

Once I saw a small spider
Creeping over leaves
What wicked traps
This little animal weaves.

Once I saw a pretty bird
Soaring across the sky
If there's one thing that fascinates me
It'd be the way they fly.

Once I saw a furry cat
Stalking its prey
It looked quite cute really
Crouching in the hay.

Once I saw a big dog
Chasing a dainty cat
The cat out sped it easily
The dog was far too fat.

Once I saw a huge giraffe
Munching on the trees
If I put my arms out straight
I could reach his knees.

David Hassan Benhenni

Sometimes

Sometimes we hurt when others we are fine
The healing we crave will be here in time
But just how much longer must we have to wait
Before the suffering we experience will get too great.

The pain just gets stronger with every day
We can't do a thing because it gets in our way
Maybe tomorrow or the day after that
We will feel much better and that will be that.

I know that there is pleasure, which we would implore
The trouble with it, is that we would crave more
So we get through the pain in our very own way
And we all live to fight another meaningful day.

With all this in mind we all do our best
To even things out whatever our quest
It's important to stay focused in times of trouble
Because if we lose it there's bound to be double.

This is the way we live out our lives
Sometimes we're sad and others surprised
But no matter what we all would agree
It's better to help you than to have you help me.

Stephen Matthews

Anchor Books – Immortal Musings

What Would You?

What would you do, what would you say
If Jesus called with you today?
Would you smile with joy as you see Him come
And welcome Him into your home?

What would He see as He entered in?
Would He feel that warmth that knows no sin?
Would the Holy Bible be there in view?
Would He feel content being there with you?

Would you want to take Him into your arms
And feel the wounds in His blessed palms?
Would you weep with sadness as you recall His pain
And see the compassion in His eyes again?

Would you run to hide in guilty shame
And whisper fearfully, 'What was His name?'
No Bible to see. No welcome 'Hello!'
Would He have to find somewhere else to go?

Don't linger no more, don't be too late,
For behold, there He stands outside your gate!
Open up your door, call Him in,
For He has said, 'I quickly come!'

Isaac Smith

The Magic Of A Smile

A smile is a priceless gift to give to everyone
Give lots of smiles to others who may have none.

With a smile you spread joy, and people feel special
It will make you happy, and is giving love to all.

To your life, you see what a difference a smile makes
So always keep the magic of a smile on your face.

When you give out smiles you will never be alone
And you can smile even when chatting on the phone.

Everywhere you go, at people keep on smiling
You could change their day from grey to dazzling.

Smiling warms people to us, as we look so friendly
Never without friends, with you others will want to be.

A smile is worth nothing until it is given away
Always keep smiling as it could make someone's day.

No words are needed when smiling, the message is there
Don't worry if others don't smile, at you they might stare.

A good that a smile can do to others, we'll never know
Don't ever forget to give smiles, everywhere you go.

A lovely smile reveals a lovely soul, an invisible beauty
No one forgets a beautiful smile, it remains in our memory.

So every day always give everyone a fabulous smile
As you will find that it will be all worthwhile.

Lindy Roberts

It's All Gone Wrong Today

(Thank you countries of European Football Cup 2004
for wonderful entertainment and passion)

It's all gone wrong today,
It's all gone wrong today,
The ball just lost its way,
Blue skies turn to grey.

It's all gone wrong today,
However hard they play,
The goals don't come their way,
It's all gone wrong today.

La, la, la, la, laa,
La, la, la, la, laa,
Da ray, da ree, da ray,
It's all gone wrong today.

The coloured flags all gay,
In gentle breezes sway,
Some hands together pray,
Save our team they say.

But it's all gone wrong today,
Each country falls away,
With distraught tears that say,
It's all gone wrong today.

Carol Ann Darling

Memories

I remember the day of your amazing birth
I remember as it filled me with bundles of mirth
I remember the day you made me cry
I remember the day as I looked to the sky
I remember the day I first heard you weep
I remember the day as I rocked you to sleep
I remember the day you first called me Dad
I remember the day as I was tearfully glad
I remember the day you took your first stride
I remember the day as your smile was wide
I remember the day you first bumped your head
I remember the day as I tucked you in bed
I remember the day I first read you a tale
I remember the day as you let out a wail
I remember the day we did wonderful things
I remember the day as we played on the swings
I remember the day we had a short race
I remember the day as we had an embrace
I remember the day we played in the sand
I remember the day as we left hand in hand
I remember the day we visited your gran
I remember the day she said you're a wee man
I remember the day the sun split the trees
I remember the day as we strolled in its breeze
Left only with these memories of you precious boy
But with so many moments that fill me with joy
One day soon you will be back with me
Oh how your dad he longs to be free.

Steven Wilson

So Sorry

The job of playing God was mine for a day
A role I hoped I'd never have to play.

I asked you to step in, cos she was one of your best
But you must have been busy or taking a rest.

You knew this would rip out a piece of my heart
And still you chose to play not a part.

She belonged to our family, loyal beyond compare
To delegate your duties, doesn't seem fair.

And the least you could do, is to just help me out
A whimper of pain to remove any doubt.

Stop her tail from wagging, take her spirit away
Just stop her from looking at me that way.

The very nature of Man lends to hope and pray
It's your life, you gave it, you take it away.

The decision was made and then nothing stirs
The tears in my eyes replaced the sparkle in hers.

So how long will I have to question my choice
Answer me now God, let's hear Your voice.

I'd have given anything if she could tell me I'm right
That she'd had enough of her valiant fight.

You can stick your job, it's the worst one I've had
It's left me hurting and grieving and sad.

'It was for the best,' seems the only way to defend
What I did today to my Cindy, my friend.

Graham Cullen

Don't Wanna

Don't wanna drive in your cities
Don't wanna drink in your bars
Don't wanna dance in your moonlight
Don't wanna swing on your stars
Don't wanna walk by the rivers
Don't wanna swim in your pools
Don't wanna piece of your action
Don't wanna bend for your rules
Don't wanna pray for your promise
Don't wanna fall for your charms
Don't wanna follow your fashion
Don't wanna lay in your arms
Don't wanna bow to your idols
Don't wanna choke on your fame
Don't wanna sing in your choir
Don't wanna part of your shame
Don't wanna wait for your verdict
Don't wanna rot in your cell
Don't wanna live in your Heaven
Don't wanna die in your Hell!

Rod Trott

A Verse For Valentine's Day

A rose is a romantic flower,
But when all is said and done;
Where a kiss is concerned, even roses admit
That tulips are better than one!

Roger Williams

Comedians

Good comedians of yesteryear,
In my mind, still appear,
Such as Reg Dixon and Max Miller,
And George Robey are laughter thrills,
I miss good clean comedy,
Which you used to hear on holiday,
I'm thirty and I'm not being shirty,
But some comedians of today are really dirty,
Mike Harding, Jim Davidson,
Ben Elton and Billy Connelly
Are to be put to the test.
Give me Victoria Wood,
Harry Hill and Phil Cool,
They're no fools,
Say goodbye to Jo Brand
As her jokes make 'choke'.

Kathy Davies-Orberson

Fate

Fickle fate paints my future black -
I have aged ten years in a day.
Yet, I am unabandoned. Instead
I am imbued with love.
It flows into me from those eyes
Like a transfusion of the spirit.
When he holds my aching body
He holds my soul, pouring in his own.
In his strength I find my own.
In his patience I find my resolve.
He has painted my future.
It is not black.

Sarah Howard

Little Grey Mouse

Little grey mouse on the kitchen table,
Better leave the building while you are able,
For my wife has seen you and vowed to kill,
With dreaded rat lime or a miniature gin.

Little grey mouse I don't wish to alarm,
And I've no desire to cause you harm,
Pay close attention to this friendly warning,
Or you won't wake up tomorrow morning.

Little grey mouse you created a stir,
The would be assassin had to jump on a chair,
So pack your belongings and scurry away,
And you'll live to steal from us another day.

Little grey mouse it was free advice,
Which you chose to ignore and paid the price,
A foolish little scrounger who refused to go,
I regret very much that it ended in woe.

G F B

Easter Bunnies

Tiny small children running all around,
Looking for treasures near the trees and on the ground.
Decorated Easter baskets,
Ribbons and coloured bows,
Lots of Easter egg bunnies,
Set out all in a row.
Tiny little feet tread softly on the grass,
Handling the little eggs as if they were made of glass.
Baskets now full,
Tired little ones go home to bed,
Dreams of chocolate bunnies,
Running around in their tiny heads.

Mary Plumb

McGuffin's Prize

In my vanity I write hung with the molly hawk of midnight,
The old superstition held in the rhyme.
I row my little boat of words upon the sea of time,
Feigning deafness to the sailors cries -
Aboard the quinquereme of dreams.
Waiting-moored-in the delta of my weary, pounding brain.

In my scrivener's crypt lie pages ripped -
Paper cradles of nascent verse - abandoned or stillborn.
The pen between my fingers has become a stinging thorn.
Plump larval thoughts are stilled - they starve and die -
Like a saprophytic stooks in forgotten fields of rye.
Whilst a milky brume begins to swirl around my *rheumy* eyes.

The stench of wasted time hangs heavy in the stygian air -
Where the sturm and drang of emotions are charged with my despair.
My wordwain stands empty - the harvest here has failed.
From the crumbling harbour of my muse the ferryman has sailed,
Away on the swell where the siren cries.
Away with McGuffin's glittering prize.

Philip J Mee

Relegation?

'Home Defeat Syndrome'
Cannot be denied -
Some football supporters
Have actually died
When their home-team
Has lost all its hope
And its pride.
When The Black Cats are down
So is Sunderland Town.
When the final score is spoken
Many a heart is broken.

Joyce Hemsley

Knock Please

You have been silent.
Your silence
hangs heavily around me
as I wait for your knock
to break in on the silence . . .
logged on.
I traverse
the silences
in search of the
faintest of whispers
that will assure me
you are fine.
But the echoes
bring in more silence.
Sharp, still
chill as death.
I can search no more.
This silence,
Blocks, hurts.

Dr Mary Annie AV (Anna Maria)

Eternal Love

I watch the sun rise, to shine another day,
Then I watch it disappear again,
To take the day away.
I listen to the waves, thrusting against the shore.
Then I watch the tide disappear,
And the night is still once more.

Oh how it feels so perfect,
Your body entwined in mine.
In the dim light of the ghostly moon,
Both oblivious to time.
This night will be over soon,
But I know your heart will always be mine.

Diane Beamish

A Sandwich

A sandwich is a funny thing,
Created by a lord.
It starts its life as a piece of bread,
Cut to shape on a board.

A sandwich is just bread,
If it has nothing in-between.
It may be filled with a lettuce leaf,
Or ham that's juicy and lean.

It can be just left open,
That means it's without a cover.
Its middle all exposed,
I think I prefer the other.

It can be fat and round.
It can be thin and square.
You take a few big bites,
And find it's no longer there.

Dorothy Foster

The Sandcastle

The sand is strewn,
the buckets flung,
the spades stand sentinel
where boys dug deep
to shape a keep
and castle adorned with shell.

Tall turrets grand
survey the sand
while upward-creeping foam
its lacy fingers,
close in, linger,
flood the majestic home.

Pandy Pond

The Lily And The Frog

The lily's scent is subtle yet holds your senses fast
but like the lily blossom her love's not meant to last
as winter sets in on the pond, her withered petals fall
the crumpled remnants of her splendour
drift off beyond recall.

But Frog, he can remember as he sits on her wilting pad
his voice once filled with love songs
is now subdued and sad.
He lays himself beside her, still wrapped in lily's fronds
his body soon decays and dies
his melody has gone.

Spring sunshine filters through the trees
to replenish the forest pond.
New shoots begin to form and sprout as lily is reborn.
Her beauty is breathtaking as she looks o'er her domain
she spreads her scent into the air to enrapture hearts again.
No thought now of springtimes gone
her memory slate's wiped clean.
She blossoms now for love anew and old ones that have been.
For old loves must remain like that
like dreams in her winter's sleep.
Already she's forgotten the frog
who died there at her feet.

George Holmes

Frontline Against Tyranny

Tragic heir to the first, the Second World War began
Dark, evil days ahead, frontline Europe then Britain
Highest praise can only extol, wondrous loyalty
To their people, the family of British royalty
King George, his lovely Queen Elizabeth, their subjects adored
Proffered haven and shelter elsewhere, they ignored
Young princesses, Elizabeth and Margaret, cheerful
                                  appearance carefree
Toiled alongside Land Army girls, encouragement for all to see
Buckingham Palace, target for the 'Hun', damp, dank dwelling then
Oh we British were fortunate, our royalty, air force boys and men
The Battle of Britain, by air, for our island, saved the day
Grieving hearts, soldiers, sailors, allied forces, worldwide saved
                                  horrendous foray
By frontline, land and sea and air
D Day ruse foiled 'Gerry' over there
We must not forget, nay allow any to forget
Multitudinous lives lost for the freedom we beget
War is unholy, evil, still, today, sacrifice precious lives lost
Western civilisation, democratic free at such cost
Symbolic of British war heroes, our Queen's regal reign
Personal problems aside, she appears time and again
Exemplary, a born queen, we are proud for the world to see
Long live Queen Elizabeth II, Regina as a queen should be

Christina Craig Harkness

Skills Of Love

Essential nature based in time
Bound I am to go
Poet in Society
Lay me down in a bed of roses

Quick gunfire over my head
Lay me flat on the ground
Love skills thrills
Who fired the first round?

Love skills of an international quality
Equality for you, love skills for me
Lay it on thick as your fist
Skills just as good as yours, mate

Enough to last until the end of time
When the poets run out of rhyme
Or people fear to speak your name
Love skills just like the rest of them

Invade me in your darkest hour
Even though you hold a terror
Of love skills strong like ice, like fire
Believe it, possess me with your skills of love -
Eternally:

Stella Thompson

Kindness Returned

When I was a boy many years ago
I had dreams I couldn't fulfil
I was oh, so small and very weak
And I was seriously ill
I never thought of having a life
That would last such a long, long time
But I had friends who were kind to me
In the end I was feeling fine
I won't forget all my friends
In times when life seemed bad
For if they could see me now
They wouldn't feel so sad
But in these days much later on
And we are growing old
The passage of time has caught us up
And has taken a heavy toll
So call on me my bosom friends
And I'll be by your side
I'll be there to help you
And I will be your guide
So take my hand be not afraid
Of the times that lie ahead
For there will be much happiness
With no more fear or dread

Frederick Thompson

Going Over

We're going over lads
At break of day,
We're going over lads
Come what may,
This muddy field we'll leave,
Far behind,
Come what may my lads,
Our fate is signed,
Fix your bayonets lads,
Tread with care,
Give your all my lads
Give your share,
When in the end my lads
They will say,
A few more feet my lads,
Another day,
We're in God's hands
And in the end,
Each one of us, will lose
A friend,
Shell-shocked, named,
For cowardice sake,
In innocence their voices break,
And those the loved ones,
Left behind,
Will carve those young lads',
Names with pride.

Maxwell Dunlop

Saying Goodbye

I'm sorry for these words I say,
It isn't fair for me to stay,
You're better off, you can move on,
You'll soon recover when I'm gone.

I'm sorry for the times I lied,
But don't you know I really tried.
You thought that things could stay the same
But not with your friend in the game.

I'm sorry for the hurt I've caused,
I'm sorry you have come off worst,
I'm sorry our love didn't last,
I'm sorry you are now my past.

We had our good times before the bad
And for those times I'm truly glad,
The memories I will keep inside,
I didn't mean to hurt your pride.

You introduced your friend to me,
From then on we were always three,
Out together enjoying life
Until the fun had turned to strife.

Couldn't you tell when things went wrong?
Couldn't you see I tried to be strong?
Don't you see we had to part
When Johnny smiled and stole my heart?

Doris Green

To Anguila

Through sapphire, turquoise shining seas
Magic sails with perfect ease.
Warm sun on face and wind through hair,
Force eight here; beyond compare.

Flying fish across the bows
Glistening, shimmering, their short flight.
Sea sounds lull the senses now
Till that next wave throws its might

Soon this idyll will not be mine,
A frigate bird I see,
Ahead Anguila, white sands shine
I wish this were eternity.

Diane Frampton

Two World Wars

Two world wars we've been through
Two world wars they died
Husbands, sons and grandads
No longer by our side

Two world wars of fighting
Two world wars they fought
No longer to walk on this Earth
But always in our thoughts

Two world wars of trenches
Two world wars of pain
They fought and died that we might live
Now we're at war again

Grace Divine

Lost And Found

I still love you so much,
it feels like I can't breathe,
I still miss you so much,
you wouldn't believe,
if your aim was to hurt me,
you've done it well,
just letting you know you succeeded,
it feels like I've climbed Mount Everest,
and then fell,
all I wanted was for you to love me,
looks like I asked for too much,
we were so good together,
I miss your soft touch,
sleepless nights and endless pain,
from my hurt I wonder,
what has he gained?
It's hard living without his love in my heart,
I try so hard to keep it together,
but really I'm falling apart,
I want to leave all this heartache behind,
I'm fed up with counting these tears of mine.

Katie Mason

First Snowdrop

Little snowdrop in my winter's garden
I spied you there today,
Your pure white petals and tiny green bonnet,
Danced with a gentle sway.

How beautiful and perfect
God's creation small and fair,
He sent you first to tell us
Another spring is in the air.

Dorothy M Mitchell

First Love

First love - in infants' school at five
When our penny milk we shared
Our little coat racks side by side
Yours pictured by an elephant, mine by a ladybird

Infants into junior school
Saw your life and mine entwine
Till up loomed the dread 11-plus
And nineteen thirty-nine

And then I failed the Grammar School
To Canada you sailed away
And though you did return once more
You brought your fiancée.

W R Probert

UK Lifestyle

The rush to work, the struggle home,
The never silent mobile phone,
And when the weekly grind is done,
Then 'garden rivals' we become,
Where once stood lawns, or fruit and veg,
Now stainless steel and trim box hedge.

Indoors the mood is much the same,
From space the 'house invaders' came,
With crimson walls and spot-lit floors
Don't forget the lime-green doors.
So much to do, so little time,
Our social life is in decline,
'All work and no play, makes Jack a dull boy,'
So they say.

Mark L Moulds

Anchor Books – Immortal Musings

Beyond The Boundary

You sat on a chair
inside my head,
a lock and key
where your mouth used to be.
Maze after maze,
grown by you,
will I burn them?
I don't think so.
You buy coffee by the pound,
upside down, around and around,
I try to keep myself awake,
your heartbeat all too fake.
We are left with nowhere to run,
nowhere to hide.
Now, I'm in a virgin state of mind.

Antony G Sarno

Missing You - Let's Meet Again!

Having first met Clare and John
Now very dear friends
Some years before
How nice we were able to meet
Weston-Super-Mare, February 2004
Again once more
A holiday we'd arranged together
Perfectly planned, went just grand
Hope not too long before
Our friends we meet once more.

Rosemary Sheridan

Summer Days

The Old English Garden in the parkland at Sewerby
Is always a most wonderful place to be,
Through the seasons of autumn and winter and springtime
Yet summer's the loveliest time for me.

The beds are aglow with flowers so fair
Surrounded by miniature hedges of box
All trimmed so neatly, enhancing each plot
Of pansies and primulas displaying their frocks.

The colours glow brightly in summer's warm sunshine
There's a great sense of peace pervading the air.
This walled garden of old is a haven of treasure
With birds, bees and butterflies everywhere.

It's a place to dream dreams, and it's not hard to see
Crinolined ladies with parasols shading their faces
Promenading the pathways beneath the rose arches,
Or resting in arbours in shadowy places.

The summers of ages past meet with the present
In this haven of quiet beauty and peace,
For the beauty and colours of nature will ever
Progress through the seasons till time itself cease.

Barbara Dunning

I Love You

I love you like no other,
You remind me of my favourite flower,
Roses are red and full of love,
And you are like one big glove,
Always keeping me warm and cosy,
And telling me to stop being so nosy,
Now this is a poem from me to you,
To let you know how much I love you.

Carol Smith (11)

Incomplete

My life is so desolate and incomplete without you around, my love

Of course I knew it would not be full, brimming over with happiness and laughter but I could not have foreseen just how empty and barren it would become.

You were my life and now all that remains is a huge hole that you once filled. I am a jigsaw with a missing piece, the most important piece, you

My mind is numb, time drags and every step requires a great effort, an effort for which I have very little energy or enthusiasm left.

My heavy heart beats on in desperate hope for you, cries and screams out for your presence every day and night. It has chosen you and will accept no one else

Problem is, because I still love you, my life remains on hold, I cannot move on

So, until you feel the same, if you ever do, I will remain incomplete, hoping that, one day soon, you will bring happiness and joy back to my life and make me a complete human being once more . . .

Nash

On T

You have never been able to question yourself
You are, most admirably, constant as the Northern Star
(To whom both distant and fixed qualities can be attached)
You are Apollo, Eros or some other tragic beauty come to Earth
You are Napoleon and Arthur or Lancelot, take your pick
You've heard of the apple that astonished Paris?
You are the stone that tripped Aphrodite,
You are the philosopher that moved the poet.

Emerson Richards

Love Is All

We've been married
just one year.
There's no reason
we should fear.

And, oh,
we've got the sweetest things.
Things that
money cannot bring.

We've got love
and understanding.
Away with ego,
and no demanding.

We've got it all
in our nest.
Love and happiness
and all the rest.

That fills our hearts
with bliss.
It's the cutest thing
there is.

Francis Xavier Farrugia

Minted Manners

'Fancy a mint Grandpa? Fancy a mint?'
It isn't asking, is it?
Mummy says it's rude to ask
She's often taking me to task
But I didn't say, 'May?' or even, 'Please'
Nor, 'Could I?' No! Not any of these
I was polite and only hinted
About sweets that are so nicely minted
So I'm sure she'll excuse me if I say,
'Fancy a mint Grandpa? Fancy a mint?'

When I am getting in his car
It really isn't going too far
To mention the fact and make it plain
That I fancy a mint - just once again
He's never refused, I must confess
I always get one - that is - unless
My meal is due and then it's true
I get one for after, or maybe two.
I often wonder - if it's fair
He doesn't seem to get his share
But should I wonder? Should I care?
'Fancy a mint Grandpa? Fancy a mint?'

R W Meacheam

Spring All The Way

A pleasant evening of spring,
Invited my heart to dance and sing.
And far beyond the valley I could see,
Clouds scarping mountaintops, with glee.

A blurred figure with arms wide spread,
Across the floating clouds, I could see ahead.
My heart missed a beat; I longed to meet him,
But he was gone, leaving streaks of sunrays and
                        an evening dull and dim.

The next day I went up and waited there,
But there was no sign of him anywhere.
Disappointed, when I got up to return,
A pleasant fragrance fill the place and for one last time
                        made me turn.

There before my eyes he stood,
His golden hair perfectly blending with his hood.
His eyes, dark and deep as the sea,
Could overshadow the night just as they had overpowered me.

He then asked for my hand, going down on to his knees,
This perfect scenario was completed by fragrance and music,
                        brought in by the breeze.
In this new world of ours, time just flew,
Soon the day would come for me to leave, 'cause I didn't belong
                        here; he knew.

Finally, the day came for us to part,
The tears in our eyes spoke of the immense grief in our heart.
He then embraced me, in a hug so tender,
That even the clouds closed in, to bond us forever.

The whistle of the train nearly drew us apart,
My legs turned to leave, but there still stood my heart.
The train began to leave yet I stood there,
And turned back forever, to gaze into his eternal stare.

His dark eyes filled with tears, now looked blue,
He locked me in his arms and said, 'I love you!'

Tina Celia

The Squeedly Tweedler

The Squeedly Tweedler had flolloping flippers
which fitted quite neatly in fluffy blue slippers.
Simply adapted to searching for food;
a strangety, willoping, flibberry dude.

His passion, his fashion, was bilberry pie,
and oh for a snifter he'd happily sigh.
Squeedly Tweedler would fargle and blither;
To the bilberry bush he'd slantily slither.

But ne'er on a Monday and ne'er in June,
would the Squeedly Tweedler, a bilberry, prune.
For bilberry had to be purply ripe,
or the Squeedly Tweedler's tummy would gripe.

He picked them and snicked them and slabbered in glee,
and frugally baked some in pastry for tea.
Then Squeedly Tweedler would off with his trove
and slantily slither to Niggaly Grove.

There he would trade with Bimble O' Nimble
for Flimberry ale, purveyed by the thimble.
Bimble O'Nimble was blighty and bleer;
he often wore hats through which he would peer.

Bimble O'Nimble would scaggle and skeek
for many a mile, to Flimberry seek.
Now oddly in June, his fare would abound,
and only on Monday was easily found!

But all became clear for their prize was the same
'Bilberry', 'Flimberry', what's in a name?

So Squeedly Tweedler and Bimble O'Nimble
their pie and their ale (purveyed by the thimble),
it seems were in tune (their tastes much alike),
did gobble and gibble and cheer with a shrike!

Martin S Colclough

True Love

Between the sorrow and the pain,
Joy has filled my heart again,
Which so long had empty lain,
For I have found true love.

A passion that is never-ending,
Fallen spirit's now ascending,
From my soul to her I'm sending,
All of my true love.

To have someone to comfort me,
To lift me from my misery,
And knowing that she'll always be,
My saviour and true love.

To see the clouds now roll away,
And sunlight shining where I lay,
I feel reborn upon this day,
The day I found true love.

A Blakemore

Waiting, Waiting

The pain of waiting is hard to bear,
Eyes red from weeping, faces grey with sorrow,
Friends and family, loved ones who share
The hours of grief for news
Which does not come, waiting, waiting.

Memories flit across the mind in sad remembrance,
A long look at treasured snapshots,
Tears running down track-ridden cheeks,
The pain of loss so great
Will it never end, this waiting, waiting?

Plans for the future so readily made,
What now no future, a grey cloud instead,
Children left motherless, families, no husbands,
The loved ones are gone, hearts broken,
Pitiless emptiness, waiting, waiting.

Elizabeth Hiddleston

Simply Sport

I'm fed up with tennis and football
Can't wait for the season to end
So things can get back to normal
Like working and phoning a friend.

It's not just the actual matches
That draw from me hysterical screams
It's the constant inquests, replays and highlights
That keep coming like nightmarish dreams.

Then there's cricket, golf and athletics
Plus motor racing, snooker and chess,
And later on will come the Olympics
In case you're not yet under stress.

Yes, I'm fed up with tennis and football
And there's many more who feel the same.
Well, it's nice to see you and speak of it all
But please excuse me or I'll miss the game!

Betty Nevell

She Lost Her Way

No more pain, no more hurt
We'll finally have our Lee
She will leave behind
The dirty drugs
And a den of iniquity

She's finding her way
She's finding her soul
She's finally found herself

She's lost no more
She's found her way home
Thanks to God
It's what she deserves.

B Forman

Aspects Of Summer

Azure blue skies caped with fleecy clouds drifting by
Barbecues and picnics, darting swallows, skylarks sing as they
soar on high
The sea, scintillating sun diamonds, the ozone of the air as you
laze on the shore
Watching gulls swishing, children at play, yachts gaily tacking,
teatime at four
The dapple of sunshine as it filters through trees
The whispering rustle of leaves at a touch from a breeze
Embracing blissful warmth from a high summer sun
Relax with a book in the garden when your chores have been done
Admire the wondrous hues of flowers as their petals unfold
The spectrum of sunsets from turquoise to flame beautiful clouds
rimmed with gold
Hush comes of an evening, birds fly to their nests
For just a few moments, mystical silence, Earth seems to rest
Midnight blue of a night sky, stars so near twinkling bright light
A magical ethereal silvery moon, serenely gliding through the night.

Marjorie Leyshon

Springtime

In springtime, in springtime,
birds make nests and sing.
In springtime, in springtime,
baby lambs are born.
In springtime, in springtime,
we can play all day.
In springtime, in springtime,
pink and white blossom falls.

Rebecca Porter (6)

In Love With A Stranger

(For Mat)

I could drown in your deep green eyes,
Swim in a sea of my dreams
Where everything is how I want it to be,
Where I can cover up all the lies.

Somewhere relaxing, somewhere free,
Somewhere where it's just you and me
On an island after dark,
On a balcony staring out at the sea,
Or strolling in the park.

You and me together
Is all my mind processes
But the sea's too rough,
The journey's too tough,
It's not worth the trouble,
The danger
Of this raging sea
And of falling in love with a stranger . . .

Leighanne Adele Smart

A Book

I'll write a book of verse
For you, my love
To show my heart is true
I'll wrap it up in finest silk
As I present it to you
And as you read the words inside
Those that poured from my soul
You shall know me more
And how much I love you
And if my prayers are answered
You shall love me too.

Matthew Holloway

Busy Buzzy Bees

A busy bee, a buzzy bee,
He buzzes near, too near to me,
Buzzes my ears, buzzes my face,
I fear I'll have to leave this place.

I don't like bees and it's not funny.
No use to me, I don't like honey.
They buzz around, near me, near you.
They land upon my Irn Bru.

It is so sweet, sweeter than buns
But it's *my* treat, I like it tonnes.
I want it back, back from the bees.
I plead with them, I'm on my knees.

They buzz angry, they buzz loud,
Of angry bees there is a cloud.
And now there's nothing I can do.
It seems I've lost my Irn Bru.

The buzzing grows, and grows, and grows!
An angry bee buzzes my nose!
And now my picnic is no fun.
I give it up and run, run, run!

John Lyons

I Will Make You See

I just don't understand,
After everything you've put me through,
I'm still here,
Crying over you,

Everything used to be great,
In fact, perfect at first,
But my dad didn't approve,
So things got even worse,

'He's not good enough for you,' he said,
'He is throwing his life away,
He will ruin your life,
And you're the one who is going to pay.'

I just couldn't take it,
So I ran away,
And my dad, as always, was right,
I was the one who had to pay,

Never fall out with your parents,
Over something that will never be,
And hopefully after reading this,
I will have made you see.

Jessica Copland

Benji

Benji is a little dog,
Who never went to school.
He just sits upon a log,
To use it as a stool.

As Benji sits and looks around,
He sees a juicy bone,
Lying there upon the ground.
He picks it up and takes it home.

Benji found it soft to chew,
The bone was extremely light,
To him it was something rather new,
For he couldn't get a bite.

Rubber it was made of,
But, Benji didn't know.
He was such way out a duff,
For to school he didn't go.

Now off to school does Benji go,
And sets off on his own,
For he's very keen to know,
About a rubber bone.

Benji learnt it's not to eat,
It's nothing but a toy,
Then he had a super treat,
A meaty bone, what joy.

Benji now is very bright,
Learning what is new,
For now he knows wrong from right,
And picks what he can chew.

D Kirk

Mollingey Stream In Spring Flood

The Molingey stream is such a wonderful scene,
as it meanders to Pentewan and the sea.
The buzzards fly high,
in this mid-Cornish sky,
just a glint of sun on a wing.
Here wildlife you can share, without a care,
Let's all know, as people, we are *free!*

The river's in spate, even though spring is late,
The ducks are still building their nest.
White-throated dipper acts the clown,
And *just nearly* gets his feet wet!
On aphids he feeds, and bits of weed,
As he flits from stone to stone.

By riverbank side, a heron is espied,
it's anyone's fish, that he'll take.
Gaudy-feathered jay, with a lopping flight,
is looking for his dinner, in the now bright sunlight.

Then just as quick as that, the weather turns black,
a clap of thunder, lightning rents the sky.
Mother Nature warns her people,
a deluge is nigh.

Down sheets the hail, and life-giving rain,
back into the river to drain.
Dusk is now starting to show,
so it's homeward we all must go.
But to get there safe, it is care we must take,
it'll be muddy all the way back,
but, *'Oh, that Cornish fresh air!'*

G J Von-Heizon

Imagination

Harry Potter, Peter Pan, Winnie the Pooh
And Tigger too
'Lord of the Rings', 'Elves and Gnomes'
All mythical creatures in children's homes.

They need to read and feel the plot
Be part of the story
They will gain a lot
Reading aloud or by themselves
Of goblins, dragons, hobbits and elves.

Going places, forests and castles
Dungeons, dragons, ships and battles
Explore, adventure, this new world is yours
It's inside the book,
You can explore from indoors.

Mystical worlds full of incredible creatures
Goblins, elves, fairies with delicate features
Giant spiders with bony legs and horrible fangs
Slimy things with slobber that hangs
From inside their mouths down to the ground.

The imagination should not be constrained
Let it loose, it won't be restrained
It's full of wild and wonderful things
And the joy of release and all that it brings
Brought forth from a child's imaginings.

Jacqui Beddow

Hedgehogs

(For Lewis)

Down at the bottom of your garden, if you look close, you'll see
A little hedgehog family living underneath the tree.
They creep about at midnight, whilst you are fast asleep
And forage in the autumn leaves that Dad left in a heap.
Searching for delicious snacks, like snails and beetle bugs
Sniffing out the juiciest worms and super slimy slugs.
Following lots of tiny footprints, they find centipedes that hide
And by lifting up a stone or two, detect where woodlice do reside.
Climbing on top of the old shed roof, they spy a hornet's nest
And scamper rather quickly down so as not to spoil their rest.
For the hornets are like angry wasps if they don't get their slumber
And have a nasty sting in their tail hedgehogs don't want

to encumber.
Now the spider's web is a favourite place to seek out food supplies.
It's full of nutritious titbits like aphids, moths and flies.
After the hedgehogs have eaten their feast and there is nothing

else to do
They look about with mischievous grins, now what can they

get up to?
When you hear scratching at your back door, please ignore their

crying pleas.
For they may be cute and pretty things but they're always covered

in fleas.
I'm sure that in an hour or two, they'll go back to sleep
Because the sun will be arising and they'll hear your alarm

clock bleep.

Night-night, little hedgehogs!

Juju

The Dawning

We hope one day that we shall see
a world that once was meant to be.
No tares that grow amongst the wheat.
So green the grass beneath our feet.

Tall trees that reach up to the sky.
Flowers that bloom and never die.
Deserts to blossom as the rose,
where fish now leap as river flows.

Purple shadows 'neath stars that gleam.
The tranquillity of a moonlit scene.
A golden sunrise lights the way
of yet another peaceful day.

The seasons changing as before,
ever obedient to nature's law.
Swallows return in early spring.
Woodlands and fields with birdsong ring.

A beautiful world once more to see.
Warfare and strife, no more to be.
Forgotten, mankind's fall from grace.
Earth's rebirth to a perfect place.

Greta Gaskin

The Autumn Of My Years

Is this my dressing table I see before me?
Anti-wrinkle creams and pungent rubs for my knee.
Fluffy balms, delicate perfumes no longer tarry,
drops for tired eyes, creams for ageing skin I marry.

Happy days when I applied Ponds' vanishing cream
and slipped into a size ten just like a dream.
Then it took a few minutes to dress for the ball,
now I need a week's notice to answer the call.

Back then, in my stilettos, I could dance all night,
gay abandon on the floor, as I took flight.
These days, painful arthritis, has tamed my feet,
after a twirl, I can do no more than take a seat.

From size ten to 16 over the years I've grown,
I've put on pounds, causing my vital joints to moan.
Who needs their tummy tucked? Who needs a facelift?
No, I need a body transplant, please make it swift.

Passing time is humbling, lost opportunities make you mad,
many joyous times have more than outweighed the bad,
My three-score years and ten have been memorable,
my life's rich tapestry still remains, indomitable.

Marian Cutler

Dedicated To Nan

(Passed away 25th December 1997)

I know I shouldn't cry, Nan,
But it's hard to fight away the tears,
When you've lost someone you love,
It's hard to say goodbye, Nan.

Although I know you're at peace now,
I can't help being selfish,
And wish you were here.
I know I shouldn't cry, Nan,
And I know what you'd say,
'Don't go crying over me,
I'm never far away.'

So I think of all the good times,
The things you used to say and do,
My tears run dry and then I smile,
Nan, there is no one like you.

Again and again, Nan
We know we shouldn't cry
But we know you'd understand
We were all so very proud
To have a nan like you.

Thinking of you always

Love

Laura

Laura Perkins

A Memo From Nature

I carry my travel suitcase
Wherever it is I go.
But needs must be disciplined,
For of seasons there shall be four.

I open my case in the springtime
Where the young shoots lift from their seeds.
Beginning their onward journey,
To a fulfilment of eventual needs.

I open my case wide in the summer,
When all fruits of life I avail.
And pastures are high from endeavour,
It pleases if not one should fail.

My summer song is long in mellowing,
Towards my autumn charisma of gold.
As I slowly begin to shut the case,
And my weather turns crinkly to old.

I close my case fully come winter,
And then I open it for all things anew.
But musts I carry new stock in my case.
So sometime obsolescence will mean you.

It is tender within my nature,
To hope you've enjoyed your stay.
I regret I can't let you linger on
God rules, I simply work for my pay.

Elwyn Johnson

Winter's Over

Spring, spring, it has a ring, that little word spring,
it means warmer weather and purple heather,
daffodils of yellow and feeling mellow,
blossom on trees and the scent of sweet flowers
cannot be spoiled by the odd April shower.
It's worth being roused by the chorus of dawn,
when the birds sit on a freshly cut lawn.
We can walk in the woods, lane and park,
climb hills with the children and be home before dark,
and if we're lucky, sit outside,
with a glass of wine and more beside,
because there is no hurry for spring to go,
and no more worry, this is nature's show.
And if you look out you might even get
the best light show, a gorgeous sunset.

Rick Oak

A Need For Love

My need for love, has been my life
It was the cause of all my strife
Fate took my mother from me, away
And ever since that dreadful day
I have always searched in vain
To find that perfect love again.
As a child, that seed was sown
But now that I am fully grown
Dear Mother, now I can see
There will never, ever be
A love so dutiful and free
As the wonderful love, you had for me.

J R Griffin

Sweet William

My father-in-law, whose name was Bill,
Was a man who loved life and its people.
He was gruff and kind and caring and true;
A real gentle man through and through.

He loved his garden, his vegetable patch,
His fruit and flowers and land.
And never got tired of showing us all
The peas and the corn and the plants growing tall.

Whenever we went to visit,
He wouldn't mow the lawn.
So the left-alone daisies would grow tall
And our children made daisy chains for us all.

We gave a bunch of Sweet William once;
My mother-in-law said it all.
She laughed as she sorted the flowers through
And said, 'Why Bill, they must be you!'

Glenys Chapman

Nature's First

Little buds peeking, finding their way
Bright colours nudging at winter's grey.
Echoes of birdsong filling the air
Seasonal promise for all to share.
The tree bare no more now starts to grow
Stands tall as she shows off nature's new clothes.
Gentle cool breezes escort the way towards the
Summer's sunshiny days.
Spring season's alarm clock now calls the time
Preparing all for the next one's prime.
Bushes and hedgerows dusted with dew
Assist the procedure of spring's life anew.
Wake-ups are nicer, evenings lighter
This gift from nature makes our lives brighter.

Virginia Aggett

Dad's Day

I'm a dad and a grandad,
But nobody will write for me,
So I'll write myself about my dad,
Setting his memory to this page,
Setting his memory free.

Dad, it's a long time since last we met,
It's years, but feels like yesterday,
For thirty years you have been in Heaven's care and scope,
So swift and sudden was your exit,
That we, your descendants, were left without a hope,

We took ages to get over the shock of losing you,
Found it difficult, no, near impossible, to accept our plight,
But we are what you made us to be,
So we knuckled down and lived our lives,
But your memory has rarely been far from our sight,

Sometimes on quite early sunny mornings,
I wonder what you'd make of your sons and daughter,
If you could come back and see us now,
Your grandchildren, your great grandchildren,
Where they live, and what they are doing,
Busy being them, giving and taking no quarter,

But I suspect, from deep, deep inside,
That you, Dad, are watching us, keeping an eye,
You know who is who, what is what, watching from the wings,
I don't think you are ever far from your family,
That's the feeling I have, can't explain the wherefores or the whys.

So for me, your eldest son,
My life follows its path, plays out its scene,
I'm fifty-eight, going on seventeen,
Overall, life's been kind to me in so many different ways,
And it's thanks to you, dear Dad, that we can all realise our dream.

P J Littlefield

Late May Again

My love, once more we find ourselves towards the close of May,
the Earth, between two seasons poised, before it breaks away,
as if suspended, nature waits, reluctant to let go,
to say farewell to springtime's charm and greet the summer's show.

Although the spring's departing hand clings to its fading past,
all sense that June's hot bloom-filled blaze is now approaching fast,
as plates of musky elderflower in perfumed cream break out,
that brighter, warmer days draw near, we know, there is no doubt.

Whilst blossomed hawthorns slowly shed their gentle wedding white,
the dew-steeped grass, confetti-strewn, takes on a rueful sight,
likewise the lilac's sun-dried plumes, brown, hanging on the tree,
above the verge where dandelions float moons opaque and free.

Once fragrant cowslip heads, now spent, straw-hatted,
                                        hang and sigh,
lamenting their fresh yellow youth beneath late April's sky,
but, waiting, straining, yet to bloom, the ready rosebuds swell,
and purpling foxgloved fingers stretch within the shaded dell.

. . . For me, such longing May days hold a special quality,
they mark the time, one year ago, which saw my heart break free,
on that late, sun-warmed afternoon our separate paths first met,
and what my yearning soul then found, I never shall forget,

Such beauty and such gentleness, how deeply they moved me,
but I sensed, too, that we did share a strong affinity,
our common bonds, our friendship true, have come to mean
                                        so much,
my heart, once like a rosebud closed, now blossoms with your touch.

For you, my love, have wrought a change, I still feel deep inside,
my life, in springtime's simple past, no longer can abide,
you've made my world like June's fair month, rose-scented,
                                        bright and new,
but . . . while I live, I'll love late May, that time I first found you.

Nick Cox

Free

As I stroll along the sandy beach
The warm golden grains embrace my feet

I can see the ship drifting in the distance
The sea so peaceful while the sun is glistening

A perfect picture on a summer's afternoon
The small fishing boats set off from the lagoon

A gentle breeze whisks through my hair
I walk further along because I know you are there

As I sit upon a rock near shore
Up above I look to see an eagle soar

I look around and it's nowhere to be seen
Then suddenly it perches next to me

After what seemed like forever sitting happily there
The eagle flew gracefully into the sweet-smelling sea air

I look above towards the sky so blue
And I knew at that moment, the golden eagle was you.

Nicola Pierce

Anchor Books – Immortal Musings

A Summer Cocoon

The small statue of St Francis stands in a corner
A tiny bird held tenderly within his protected hand
Shades of sunlight filter through the leafy fauna
A warm breeze in the air seems to be softly fanned

Wonder nature's beauty of a lovely summer's garden
White blossom of camellia, flowers of many a shade
Perfection perfect beyond creation of a poet's pen
The sweet fragrance of roses each petal an accolade

Well-tended lawns and borders to give sheer delight
A variant coloured lush green ivy-covered wall
Apple and pear trees laden, their fruit ready to ripe
In amongst the rich vibrant bushes and bowers so tall

So often it is said that the Lord is to be found in such a place
Yet not really too hard to understand the reason why!
It's the feeling of a peace far away from life's great race
A serene time put aside for thinking and dreaming, if we try

Then it sends out the message of tranquillity in a cocoon
A spot where your heart and soul can securely attune.

Octavia Hornby

Stories Of War

The soldiers who fought
Remember it well,
They always have a story to tell.
The good times, the bad,
Happy and sad,
Oh, how they remember it well.
The sad thing is, their stories don't last
Only in memories of loved ones
To whom it was passed.
We all need to listen
While we still can - to the stories of war
From these very special men.
To remember is the right thing to do
They all fought for our country,
For me - and for you.

Helen Dakin

Untitled

When the Twin Towers in New York hit the ground
A whole world was visibly shaken
A million lost souls cried to God,
'Tell us why have You left us forsaken?'

Devastation and despair did abound
Surrounding that hole in the ground
Then people of words
And political nerds
Said, 'It's now time to turn things around.'

When the dust and the debris was shifted
No memory could ever be lifted
They all will, with sadness, remember
That terrible day in September.

M Saye

Salt Of The Earth

My dear old dad was born today
On the fifteenth day of May
I know if he were still around
He would be digging up the ground
Planting runner beans and beet
Fruits and veg for us to eat
Rhubarb, lettuce, onions too
Anything at all, he grew
His wallflower bed, a lovely sight
And scented stock, came out at night
Lupins tall, rose-pink and blue
Tulips, and nasturtiums too
And in the border, near the lawn
The feathered Prince of Wales adorn
If my dear dad were still alive
He'd be a grand hundred and five
He'll be gardening still, I know
Helping Heaven's flowers to grow.

Joan Fletcher

A Moment

A barefoot boy
On a narrowboat roof,
Sun burnishing his hair,
And dragonflies with bronzed wings
Flitting through the air.

Water shining like beaten steel.
Overhead, the willow bends.
This place has such a serene feel
And stressful damage mends.

Miki Byrne

Magnanimous Dad

Oh! Warm loving Dad who has a heart for me
Even in your human soul, you feed my heart,
With your excessive kindness and love
My body and soul rejoices each time
Your wear your heart on your sleeve for me
Your caring determines my living on Earth.

I adore the beauty and purity of your kindness
Your kindness is bright and full of goodness
Behold, a diamond and gold can't resist your kindness.
The world could pass away but your kindness is irresistible
Oh! Dad, how magnanimous is your soul
I cherish the day God created you.

I long to feel how God moulded you
You were created punctiliously not perfunctorily
When God created you, kindness fell from Heaven
I thank the angel who bestowed you kindness
I cherish your milk of human kindness
I will take a shine to your caring.

I know that honey is sweet,
But your caring is sweeter than honey
O' magnanimous Dad, who walks in humility
So lovely, so precious and calm in gentility
Which Heaven knows with all adoration
And I love you dearly with admiration.

Arharhire Sunday

Gone In December '74

Father's Day is fast approaching just like my age
It is a time when you rejoice and also savour
All the good things you have shared with Pater

The walks along the canal, during the first days of spring
The sounds of laughter when watching 'Hancock's Half Hour'
There are so many things that we share with our father

Our first bike ride holding the handlebars so tight
When given the push, as you wiggle across the grass
You imagine how wonderful your father really is

The first time you kick the football with him in the park
The stories he would tell when sitting alone in the dark
And not forgetting how he held me so close and tender

And as you grow, that first kiss with your girlfriend
When you take her home hoping that he will like her
These are the great things about having a loving father

Well, why do I wish I could change the passing of that August?
When Father passed away, for no tear have I yet shed?
But the life I had I remember, those slaps to my head

He wasn't all bad, we did have some good times but they
Always involved alcohol and clubs, Mondays missing from school
You know I hated Christmas. For he did his best, but I cried

As the oldest I grew too fast, became the father to them
My younger brother and sister, Mam had gone in December '74
But I guess the one true thing that I miss is the survival.

Kieth T Jones (Roker)

A Hanky With An 'E'

A hanky with an 'E' means my daddy:
The little things that bring him back to me:
Listening to his witty poem or story
As I sit near him or upon his knee.
Racing down the road at his homecoming
To see his old familiar trilby hat,
His briefcase and his coat flaps waving
To catch me as I speed to hear his chat.
Him sitting at his bureau quietly writing,
His pipe and spill in rack above his head,
His drawer full of baccy-smelling papers,
His old typewriter ribbon almost dead!
The garden, where he often laboured for us,
Tending veg and flowers brightly hued,
And giving me a love of all things earthy -
The fresh air, freedom, space and solitude.
His surplice as he stood there in the chancel,
Singing in the village church in choir,
His bass voice contributing to the music,
His shoulders to the bell chimes in the tower.
A poem never can contain my daddy,
A man always so special to us all;
His loving patience and his calm acceptance,
His faith, supporting all that might befall.

Elizabeth M Jones

Counting The Clouds

Soft, rounded dunes, windswept,
With spikes of eelgrass resembling young men's chins,
Where stubborn, virgin whiskers, defying any blade.
Here, where all secrets are kept,
You are in my mind.
I search for you and wait.
What I seek,
The unattainable.

Out of reach
Never out of mind.
The noise of pounding waves,
Fills my ears
Crashing against the beach,
In the undertow smooth stones dragged against their will.
Cruel, relentless ocean.
Perpetual motion,
Reliant on the moon.
Who waits up there for the chance to woo the clouds to dance
Waltzing, to veil them in mist.
Like that first kiss
When black changed into blue,
Who was holding who?
It matters not. Mist rolling in from the sea
Was all this meant to be?

Ann Wardlaw

The Ranger

I was biting the brink of disorder
You arrived unexpectedly
Quietly and somewhat ordinary
I was ejecting toxic froth
You filled my cup with a sweet draught
It soothed my boiling veins

You preached there were no limits
Stains and flaws are there
Because we encourage them
I listened, I studied
You smoothed the chaos
And flattened my jagged seams

With a reflective narrative
You quashed my internal blemishes
Holding out your callused hand
I was mistaken
Heroes don't always announce their arrival
You crept into my lonely outpost

Now I can see flashes again
Interrupting my vexatious essence
Re-energising my lifeless force
You made me sever those
Those bleak, bestial images
Become hopeful and jubilant

This encounter restored my welfare
Made me comb and forage
For improved solutions
You are due a mound of credit
A medal should be pinned to your chest
My nomadic municipal liberator.

Sandra Lang

Thanks For Everything, Dad

He was that special kind of bloke
After making him, the mould was thrown away
He liked his pint, a cigarette and a joke
For eighty-two years, he came to stay.

He never saw the need to raise his fist
A short chat was all that was required
Some twenty years on, he is still sadly missed
A worn-out body, that had unfortunately expired.

His integrity shone through the darkest cloud
Always standing firm, beside his loving wife
Of all his children, he was extremely proud
A shining example, as I tread this path of life.

And in uniform, he fought for country and king
Called away to the dangers upon foreign soil
Such joy and laughter into our lives, he did bring
A proud man, always prepared to toil.

In quiet moments when I sit alone
Thoughts of this wonderful man come to mind
Never once did I ever see his temper blown
A more tolerant man would be hard to find.

At seventy-eight, a major operation he had to undergo
His left leg had to be removed, by amputation
To myself, in stature, he continued to grow
Though it left him in an impossible situation.

After a stroke, he was still sound of mind
Closing my eyes, I can still see the man's pain
To the nearby hospital, he was then confined
Our enormous loss was Heaven's gain.

I remember him in golden days
On winter nights, he'd blow away the cold
Anecdotes of his life, our eyes would blaze
A man with a heart of gold.

B W Ballard

My Dear Father

Abba, you were the great dad.
You gave me joy and hope.
You taught us all good deeds.
Our thoughts are of you with love.
Your guidance we remember.
It makes our lives easier.
I have always tried to follow your advice,
Your wonderful ways.
The great times together.
The fond memories, dear Father.
They will never die.
They will remain in our hearts.
You are sleeping peacefully
Under the flowered trees.
Silent, calm and gentle.
Birds are singing sad songs.
Cool breeze whispering, prays.
The sun spreading gentle rays.
We will meet you one day again.

Bilquis Giasuddin

Change

Quiet the heart,
That once beat fast with joy,
And who can say what time employed,
To break the bond that love had formed,
Before despair upon it stormed,
Absent, heartless, so it seems,
Love exists in useless dreams,
Which ended when the cold wind blew,
So who can say if love was true?

M Hughes

Describing Green To Blind Lover

Outside it lives
this restless gypsy
laughing most in spring

it summers in a field of lazy days
painting meadows for the gods
but skulks away to hide
in autumn's wrinkled skin

it sings loudest after rain
when songbirds pause to listen
licks around our ankles
when we're naked in the grass

squeeze this mint leaf in my fingers
sniff its piquant scent serene
tongue its essence on your lips
and taste me with this green

Terry R Banks

Brother Syndrome

Falling in love with someone hurts like hell,
Keeping my emotions locked in a padded cell,
As to not petrify the poor female on my mind,
Knowing that in me, she could never find,
The loving man of her dreams,
Just an image to create nightmarish screams,
'You're kind, sweet and funny,' are people's usual reaction,
And that just shows the 'brother syndrome' in action,
Their thoughts are he is nice, but you couldn't
It's really a shame but you just wouldn't,
Maybe it's something at school I did miss,
But I suppose someone has to be the 'anti-Adonis!'

Mark Redfern

Tingles

I tingle with love for the sweetest rose
that blooms eternally;
resplendent in the eyes of those
appreciative of pure beauty.
When miles divide us we communicate
in a language true lovers know.
Magical tingles will generate
the chemical forces that flow.
When I close my eyes I see her face,
in dreams she is here by my side.
Soft breezes caress me in mock embrace.
Her kisses in raindrops abide.
A guardian moon relays our thoughts
passing from one to the other.
Twinkling stars are the moon's escorts
until our return together.
I tingle with love for the sweetest rose
that blooms eternally.
Tingles may last; but loneliness grows
I want her here in reality.

Stan Coombs

The Kiss

Oh yes, I miss his tender kiss
The arms that hold
Sometimes gentle, sometimes bold
I miss the comfort and the love
I miss the goodbye kiss
The hello kiss
The loving touch that said so much
The whispered word
Quietly heard in the night
When there's little light
Oh yes, I miss the bolder kiss
The promise of so much more
The love so true, and oh, so sure!
So safe and complete
To hear his heart's crazy beat
I miss, I miss, the goodnight kiss
His tender kiss
His stronger kiss
His passionate kiss and so too
The good morning kiss
This, yes, this is what I miss!

Myra Rose Yates

Book Of Love

Open up my book of love
and you will clearly see
it's all about you, my love
And what you mean to me . . .

open up my book of love
and as you read between the lines
you'll see how much I love you
and how you're always on my mind

your hair so soft, your skin so fair
you eyes are oh, so blue
your lips are red as roses
I just can't live without you

I've never been so swept away
by beauty such as yours
you are an angel without wings
whom I worship and adore

I love being wrapped inside your arms
and your kisses set me free
if I were to die tomorrow
there's nowhere else I'd rather be

so open up my book of love
and the empty pages that you see
will be filled with love and tenderness
for you, my love, and me.

Jean Lilian Bramhill

Dream Holiday

A lovely holiday by the sea
A welcome break for you and me
I look at you with so much pride
Feeling like a blushing bride

Walking on the beach, hand in hand
Our feet are warm in the golden sand
Seagulls give out their mournful cry
Darting and diving in the clear blue sky

The laughter of children as they play
Building sandcastles with flags so gay
Surrounded by happiness we go on our way
Looking forward to another day

We snuggle up close, our arms entwine
Warmly mellowed by a glass of wine
A tender kiss, a whispered goodnight
Knowing everything will be alright

Morning dawns, life's not as it seems
My love's only with me in my dreams
He died seven long years ago
But I still love and miss him so

The wonderful times and joys we shared
Knowing that he loved and cared
Treasured memories are mine to keep
Even if it's only in my sleep.

Barbara M Beatson

Early 1939

On looking back
I see her now,
All joy from her heart had gone,
A sad and lonely figure
A victim of the Hun
A refugee from Hitler's hand.
Suffering her sorrow,
All alone.
Her loved ones she had left behind,
Never to be seen again.
Little did we realise what damage would be done.
Millions would now be lost,
Victims of the holocaust.

Overwhelming sorrow,
Exhausting tears shed.
Extermination was their loathsome work.
Humanity at *Auschwitz,*
Denied the dignity of death.

John Freeth

Voodoo Dolphin

Voodoo Dolphin has swum to me,
Now I'm living the story magically.

Rescued from my downtrodden stage,
My air crowded with animated age.

No one else has given me such love,
This voodoo dolphin fits like a glove.

Inflicting pain would break the power,
Behind the exhilarating psychedelic hour.

Permanent zest is what I required,
Aid me in the quest for my burning desire.

Harvey Aspell

Days Gone By

At times I sit and contemplate
What might have been in years gone by

Then my tired old eyes light up
When I see your sweet young face
And the sound of laughter with your vibrant grace

Would that I could join in such lively happiness
But being old, I have not the zest.

Only in thought can I now go back
And I am young once more
Did I often laugh and tease
Just to break another's heart?

Until I know, let me feel that you are real
And we must never part
When you are near, it's my only fear
Please, not too quickly, disappear!

Thomas Wylie

Precious Love

I try to show my love to you
In everything I say and do
My heart beats so when you are near
The love we share is precious and dear
To see you smile in that special way
To hear your laugh just makes my day
Your touch is like a soft caress
Your kiss is just sweet gentleness
Your arms are strong and keep me safe
When I am in your warm embrace
Your love to me is everything
It lifts my heart and makes it sing
But now you're in that heavenly place
Your absence leaves painful space.

Christine Corby

Time's Battle

Seconds tick by
On life's spinning wheel,
The hours rain down
But not one of them's real.
Days fall away,
Fading into the air,
No one will remember
Those days were there.
And the weeks and the months
Turn into the years,
And the clock on the wall
Fakes all of those tears,
For time as we know him
Is time far, far gone,
Create your own future,
And the battle you've won.

Sarah Heptinstall

April

April, the month of green leaves,
Of budding trees,
When the sun's warmth is first felt,
And last snows melt,
April, the month of blossom-pink and white,
Of migrant birds' incoming flight,
April, the month of new birth -
Replenished earth,
When woodland bell-shaped flowers,
Bloom amid the sun and showers,
April, when we hear the cuckoo's song,
A sign, that summer won't be long.

Ruth Martin

Adieu

When it's my funeral
Please don't wear black,
Don't be too sad that I'm not coming back.
Dress up in your green,
Your blue or your red,
Sing all of the hymns,
Hear all that is said.

I know we'll be parted
For perhaps many years
But quieten your worries,
And calm all your fears;
My soul will continue,
I'll be much the same,
And I will be waiting
'Til you see me again.

So embrace all the family,
Greet all of my friends,
Be assured I am with you,
For love never ends.
Go on with your journey
With Jesus as your guide,
'Til that day in the future
When we'll be side by side.

Doreen Lawrence

Pillow Talk

'Do you love me and how do you love me?' I said
As we lay in our bed,
'Are there stars in the sky?'
'Do you need to ask why?'

Jeanne E Pearce-Sagar

Ode To The Man I Love

I see him from afar,
Not minding me,
He goes off to the bar,
Oh to say the words,
I long to say,
Will he accept them?

I love him from as long as a year,
His smile, his face,
Bring me cheer, he knows me like no one else,
Listens to me moan,
Laugh and cry.

We have been there for each other all this while,
I keep my love a secret,
Would he feel the same if I said,
Or would I regret saying it
And want to be back in my bed?

How does he feel?
Does he know?
That look in his eye,
The smile on his face,
All make it harder to say,

Ode to the man I love,
He is my equal,
No one else comes above.

I get closer as time goes by,
Wishing that he was mine,
One of these days,
I will see,
What his answer would be to me,
When I tell him,
I love him so.

Suzanne Duffy

Black Or White

Life is not just black or white,
There are many shades of grey,
With sudden shafts of coloured light,
To help you find your way!

Within the maze, we call, the mind,
Hidden paths, are found,
Explore them all, in detail,
Discover sight and sound!

Approach events with caution
Some things have many sides,
Consider all the angles,
That an 'open mind' provides!

Take time, to reach conclusion,
If there is any doubt,
Listen to all argument,
Don't just rave or shout!

It's easier, to go along,
Ignoring - left or right,
But you - miss - the bigger picture,
When it's not, within your sight!

Use imagination, The -
Obvious, could, be wrong!
The world, is full of wonder,
Though feelings are strong!

See each view, in all its aspects,
Life is not just black or white,
So many shades are in-between,
No one is always - right!

E M Eagle

A Love That's Lost

Heaven is a place close by,
But nothing helps those tears to dry,
To lose someone dear does hurt so much,
No longer to hold them, nor feel their touch,
To feel such pain, to be torn apart,
Wishing to go back, to the start,
It's so hard saying goodbye,
Asking questions to the reasons why,
Why did it happen? This isn't fair,
Why is life so cruel, and left so bare?

Feeling such sorrow, so empty inside,
Countless tears have fallen and died,
If Heaven is a place so near,
Why did it take someone you loved so dear?
Why does Heaven feel so far away?
How do you live each lonely day?
Is this the price of a love that's lost?
Thoughts in your mind, muddled, all tossed,
Not knowing if you'll be complete again,
Tears falling silently, not easing the pain.

It feels like the emptiness will never fade,
Yearning for the love you both together made.
Emotions in turmoil, all gone astray.
The love you had known was taken away,
Longing inside, to see their smiling face,
And of the sadness you could not trace.
When will this sadness end? The heartache go?
This feeling of anger, when will it slow?
They say time helps, your hurt will heal.
Heaven is close by, you will surely feel.

C D Wilson

Andrew, Isabel And Madelena

Mothers' in difference make claims maternal
In the non-existence of a child's, paternal;
Dismissed as if transient, futile and sold
Fatherhood's forgotten like some rank that's gone mould.
Green-blue and hairy, infectious to touch
The prejudice of masculine is centred so much
Virility, love excitement to care
There is nothing but breakdown to prod to despair.
Such indignity pressured, inhuman and trod
Degrading in treatment as if without God.
A woman smears her campaign of lies
When her bogus ambition for custody ties
Forgetting about the children, nuisance impends
The female seething to hatred befriends.
She ousts and kills all emotion and trust
To empty expression of relationship lust.
No kisses may tell of love may then find
And relief isn't possible and time becomes unkind.
Fought in a battle, she continues to scar
Until the distance for Daddy, is ever so far.
Poor then are the sons and daughters of truth
Because of her fantasy of spite as a spoof.
What may be done, is yet to achieve
Without all the children, a dad's soul does grieve?
Planning and plotting to shoot through the brain
The menace of Mummy is never so plain
Psychology of a girl's mind, having borne her a child
Is hardened, resentful and callous, not mild.
No meekness to share, and make things just right
A dad for his children can do nothing but fight.

Anthony Rosato

There For You

I'm there for you
Whenever you call,
I'm there for you
Whenever you fall.

I'm there for you
Whatever you need,
I'm there for you
To help you succeed.

I'm there for you
Whatever the time,
I'm there for you
Through rain or shine.

I'm there for you
Whenever you're sad,
I'm there for you
To make you glad.

I'm there for you
In your despair,
I'm there for you
To show I care.

I'm there for you
Through every day,
I'm there for you
In every way.

John H Foley

Picture My Presence

(For Seyi Oshijirin)

Wherever you are,
Wherever you be,
Either near or far away
Keep our oath of love
Sacred like the Holy Communion;
Flashback at our romantic moments,
Remember our words of passion
And affection deep in emotion.
Distance reflects no difference,
You heart could picture my presence
Any time you feel my absence
And recite these words of *love:*

      Oh my dear love,
      I love you dearly
      My darling love.
      Even while I'm away,
      Whether near or far away;
      Across the widest ocean,
      Up the highest mountain,
      Down the lowest valley;
      In the depth of the deepest sea
      My heart is dearer
      To you my lonely love.
      Forever will you be my love,
      Evermore, you're my *love,*
                  Amen.

Aderemi Adegbite cfm

They Checked St Barths

'I am free, I am free
We were checked
The Government backs me!'

'Did they look at your films?
Programmes on the machine
Did they check what you really do?'

'They can't, they don't know
We talked to them so sweetly
We sound so sane to the visitor.

- I didn't know till my boys checked
That I am totally unstable
And they say Stevie is a lunatic.

Though they call it something else
Our lab was checked, we still have some dirt
They checked nothing, we're clean!'

'So you have friends in Government?'
- We have a problem, can they have stay?
They took benefits and Government wages

- And their Government pays us for this.
Hang on a minute that means . . .
Our country is not functioning at all!

Let's call it information technology
We torture then watch the results
The Princess was here, Charles too . . .

Renate Fekete

Anchor Books – Immortal Musings

Anchor Books Information

We hope you have enjoyed reading this book - and that you will continue to enjoy it in the coming years.

If you like reading and writing poetry drop us a line, or give us a call, and we'll send you a free information pack.

Alternatively if you would like to order further copies of this book or any of our other titles, then please give us a call or log onto our website at www.forwardpress.co.uk

Anchor Books Information
Remus House
Coltsfoot Drive
Peterborough
PE2 9JX

(01733) 898102